Historical Evolution of the Eastern Mode of Production

I0885219

In the four volumes of *The Development Trajectory of Eastern Societies and the Theories and Practices of Socialism*, the author re-examines Marx and Engels' theories on the development trajectory of Eastern societies by integrating theoretical analysis of Marxist theories and a historical investigation of socialist revolution and socialist construction around the world.

This second volume focuses on Marx and Engels' historical materialism, explains the general laws of historical development, and brings this to bear within the context of Eastern societies. The author notes that Marx and Engels' historical materialism and its derivative theories on Eastern societies are compatible and interconnected. In addition, he reveals how Marx and Engels' theory of the "Asiatic mode of production" plays an important part in the development trajectory of Eastern societies, and is closely related to their theory of "five social forms."

This volume is a key reference for readers who study and are interested in Marxism, Marxist philosophy, and the history of philosophy.

Jiaxiang Zhao is Professor of Philosophy at Peking University, and has served as vice dean and director of the academic committee of the Department of Philosophy, as well as vice president and consultant of the Chinese Historical Materialism Association. His main research interests include Marxist philosophy and Marxist classic works.

China Perspectives

The *China Perspectives* series focuses on translating and publishing works by leading Chinese scholars, writing about both global topics and China-related themes. It covers Humanities & Social Sciences, Education, Media and Psychology, as well as many interdisciplinary themes.

This is the first time any of these books have been published in English for international readers. The series aims to put forward a Chinese perspective, give insights into cutting-edge academic thinking in China, and inspire researchers globally.

Titles in philosophy currently include:

Secret Subversion I
Mou Zongsan, Kant, and Original Confucianism
Wenming Tang

Secret Subversion II
Mou Zongsan, Kant, and Original Confucianism
Wenming Tang

The Development Trajectory of Eastern Societies
Jiaxiang Zhao

Historical Evolution of the Eastern Mode of Production
Jiaxiang Zhao

Leaping Over the Caudine Forks of Capitalism
Jiaxiang Zhao

Theories and Practices of Scientific Socialism
Jiaxiang Zhao

The Principles of New Ethics
Volume 3: Normative Ethics II
Haiming Wang

For more information, please visit www.routledge.com/series/CPH

Historical Evolution of the Eastern Mode of Production

Jiaxiang Zhao

Translated by Qin Li

Routledge
Taylor & Francis Group
LONDON AND NEW YORK

First published 2021 by Routledge

2 Park Square, Milton Park, Abingdon, Oxon OX14 4RN
605 Third Avenue, New York, NY 10017

Routledge is an imprint of the Taylor & Francis Group, an informa business

First issued in paperback 2022

Copyright © 2021 Jiaxiang Zhao

Translated by Qin Li

The right of Jiaxiang Zhao to be identified as author of this work has been asserted by him in accordance with sections 77 and 78 of the Copyright, Designs and Patents Act 1988.

All rights reserved. No part of this book may be reprinted or reproduced or utilised in any form or by any electronic, mechanical, or other means, now known or hereafter invented, including photocopying and recording, or in any information storage or retrieval system, without permission in writing from the publishers.

Notice:
Product or corporate names may be trademarks or registered trademarks, and are used only for identification and explanation without intent to infringe.

Publisher's Note

The publisher has gone to great lengths to ensure the quality of this reprint but points out that some imperfections in the original copies may be apparent.

English version by permission of The Commercial Press.

British Library Cataloguing-in-Publication Data
A catalogue record for this book is available from the British Library

Library of Congress Cataloging-in-Publication Data
A catalog record has been requested for this book

ISBN: 978-0-367-47687-8 (hbk)
ISBN: 978-1-03-233605-3 (pbk)
DOI: 10.4324/9781003036845

Typeset in Times New Roman
by Deanta Global Publishing Services, Chennai, India

商務印書館
The Commercial Press

Contents

Introduction

Marx and Engels' historical materialism discusses the general laws of historical development. During their research on the subject, they paid great attention to the special trajectory of the development of the Eastern society. Their theory of Eastern society is an application of their theory on the general laws of social development. These two theories are compatible and interconnected, indicating a relationship between particularity and generality. The theory of Marx and Engels on the "Asiatic mode of production" and its role in social development is an important part of their theory on the development trajectory of Eastern society, and is closely related to their theory of "five social forms". This book explores (the evolution of) Marx and Engels' concept of "the Asiatic mode of production" and its role in historical development and in the theory of the "five social forms."

1 Debating the "Asiatic mode of production"

History and research methods

To properly understand Marx and Engels' concept of the "Asiatic mode of production," we need to investigate the history and research methods within the debates on this concept.

1.1 History of the debates

In 1859, Marx summed up the general development of human history in the *Preface to A Contribution to the Critique of Political Economy*: "In broad outline, the Asiatic, ancient, feudal and modern bourgeois modes of production may be designated as epochs marking progress in the economic development society."[1] Marx's concept of the "Asiatic mode of production" has a history of over 150 years. People have always debated this concept and its role in social development. It seems to be the "Goldbach Conjecture" in the disciplines of humanities and social sciences. There were two large-scale debates around the world. The first world-wide discussion from 1925 to 1931 began in the academia of the Soviet Union, followed by Japan and China. And the discussion in China's historical field continued into the 1940s. The discussion at the beginning of the founding of the People's Republic of China can be seen as the continuation of the first world-wide discussion. The first world-wide discussion focused on Chinese history, and the economic and social changes in Russia, India, Iran, Afghanistan, and other countries. The second world-wide discussion from the 1960s to 1970s involved historians, economists, philosophers, and geographers from the United Kingdom, France, Hungary, the then German Democratic Republic, Japan, Italy, Australia, and other countries. This second discussion was deeper and broader than the first. In addition to the Eastern society, the discussion also encompassed pre-colonial African society, the American society before its discovery by Columbus, and the ancient Middle Eastern societies. China's debates on this issue began after the "Cultural Revolution" and continue even today. However, controversy remains. It is no exaggeration to say that the concept of the "Asiatic mode of production" pops up in almost all philosophical, historical, and economic debates on Chinese history and its alternations in social forms.

Over the last 30 years of debate on the concept, some scholars in both China and beyond denied Marx and Engels' "five social forms," perhaps due to their misinterpretations of the "Asiatic mode of production" and its role in social history.

Some claim that the Asiatic, slave, and feudal societies are not three different economic and social forms, but three types or modes of the same social form (i.e., the pre-capitalist society after disintegration of the primitive society), coexisting simultaneously (rather than in a historical sequence) at different locations.

On the other hand, other scholars believe that after the disintegration of the primitive society, several different social forms co-existed but evolved according to different development trajectories and sequences in different countries or regions: Some Asian countries, such as China and India, entered a society of the "Asiatic mode of production"; Ancient Greece and Rome entered the slave society; and the Germanic people established the feudal society on the ruins of the Western Roman Empire. In the world as a whole, only the feudal system of Western Europe had nurtured the capitalist production relations and produced a capitalist society after the bourgeois revolution. Countries and regions outside Western Europe, especially those of the "Asiatic mode of production" as according to Marx, failed to enter capitalism. Therefore, these scholars conclude that in the world, only parts of Europe have developed in the sequence of primitive society, slave society, feudal society, and capitalist society, which is not the case in other and greater parts of the world. Consequently, these scholars claim, the theory of successive replacements of the five social forms is not universal and does not conform to historical facts.

Still, others believe that countries like China and India, in their 2,000- or 3,000-year history, from the collapse of the primitive society to their degeneration into a colony or a semi-colony after the imperialist invasions, had been a society of the "Asiatic mode of production" without going through a slave society or a feudal society.

One more group of scholars holds that only the antagonistic social formation is called the economic social form. This includes the four social forms—the Asiatic society, the slave society in Ancient Greece and Rome, the feudal society, and the capitalist society—that Marx mentioned in the *Preface to A Contribution to the Critique of Political Economy*. The primitive society and the future communist society are not antagonistic societies and do not belong to economic social forms. The four economic social forms, plus the two non-economic social forms, give humankind a total of six social forms.

Most people holding the above view assert that the theory of five social forms was not brought forth by Marx and Engels, but by Stalin in 1938 in *Dialectical and Historical Materialism*, and that it is one of the theoretical sources of dogmatism and should be negated and discarded. In this context, a systematic study of Marx and Engels on the "Asiatic mode of production" and its role in social history is theoretically and practically significant for: (1) Proper understanding of the theory of five social forms by Marx and Engels, (2) adhering to the viewpoint that historical development is governed by objective laws, and (3) comprehensive understanding of the evolution and replacement of social forms.

1.2 Cultivating correct research methods

Scholars diverge greatly in their understanding of the "Asiatic mode of production." Some consider it a primitive society; others, a slave society. Some, an oriental feudal society; others, a mixed society or prevalent slavery. One group of scholars considers the "Asiatic mode of production" an extreme form of society nonexistent in the West. The diversity of understandings here derives not only from the complexity of the concept itself, but also from the debaters' different historical perspectives and their respective historical materials and their different analytical/research methods. As different research methods may lead to different conclusions, we need to clarify certain methodological issues before our detailed discussion of the concept.

Principle one. As our first principle, an exact definition of any concept, including Marx and Engels' concept of the "Asiatic mode of production," requires us to confront modern hermeneutics. Modern hermeneutics believes that texts have no intrinsic meaning independent of the interpreter. The meaning of the text is derived from the interpreter's understanding. Different interpreters may understand the same text differently, all with justification. Modern hermeneutics concedes that even if the text has its intrinsic meaning or intention, it is inaccessible to the interpreter. The purpose of the interpreter's interpretation of the text is not to understand the original intention of the text, but to derive its meaning. Per this viewpoint of hermeneutics, the meaning of classical Marxism is dependent on the interpreter, whatever the interpretation is. Even distorted interpretations, malicious attacks, and denials have their justifications. This viewpoint of hermeneutics will inevitably negate any intrinsic meaning or intention behind classical Marxism. I contend that Marxism must be interpreted in light of contemporary social conditions and practical tasks, and the original intention of classical Marxism cannot be negated. I believe that the proper interpretation of classical Marxism needs to follow five steps:

First, we need to delve into the original intention of original texts. Any original text has its author's original intention. Proper interpretation needs to be rendered in accordance with the author's historical background and conditions, the author's own political position and academic achievement, the specific problems at the author's time, and the strict content of the text. We must not introduce into our interpretation extraneous elements, such as the background and historical conditions of the interpreter, the interpreter's preconceptions (especially prejudices unconducive to correct interpretations), and the interpreter's own understandings of the classic text. If the classic text does not have its original intention, any study of it will be meaningless.

Second, we need to differentiate between varied interpretations. Certainly, different interpreters have different and even opposite interpretations of the same text. The difference represents different degrees of conformity with the original text. Different interpretations cannot justify negation of the original meaning and intention of the author.

Third, we need to correctly evaluate the interpreter's preconceptions. The interpretation of classic texts is undoubtedly done on basis of the interpreter's preconceptions. No mind is a blank slate free of preconceptions and its own research methods. However, the effects of different preconceptions differ on the interpretation of the original text. Some preconceptions may better approximate the original text and facilitate correct understanding of it. Others deviate more from the original text and hamper the correct understanding of it. This again cannot negate the inherent meanings of the original text.

Fourth, we need to correctly assess the interpreter's critique of the classic text. The interpreter not only interprets but also critiques the original text. The interpreter may favor or oppose the original text depending on their critique of it. This again cannot negate the inherent message or intention of the original text.

Fifth, we need to distinguish between the original intention of the text and new ideas introduced by the interpreter. The interpreter should not only correctly interpret but also properly activate the original intention of the classic text, in light of the interpreter's current historical conditions and tasks. If the interpreter's new ideas added to the original text represent coherent continuation of the latter and help resolve current problems, we may claim that the interpreter enriches and develops the original text in accordance with the needs of current tasks and conditions.

Marx and Engels always opposed misinterpretation of their works. In the preface to *Capital Volume III*, on some bourgeois economists' distortions of Marx's theory of average profit rate law, Engels says:

> When a man wants to deal with scientific questions he should above all learn to read the works he wishes to use just as the author had written them, and above all without reading anything into them that they do not contain.[2]

Despite the fact that no modern Western hermeneutics yet existed when Engels said the above, methods of hermeneutics were apparently and unconsciously used. Concerning the interpretation of classic texts, I strongly agree with Engels' view rather than modern Western hermeneutics. Only under the premise that the works of Marx and Engels have inherent messages can we correctly discuss the concept of the "Asiatic mode of production" and its role in social and historical development. In order to accurately decipher this concept, we must examine the entire body of Marxist works instead of only those that support the interpreter's wishes. Nor should we use knowledge available now but unavailable in Marx's time to premise our interpretations. Otherwise, misinterpretations easily arise. Researchers of the "Asiatic mode of production" often diverge on their understanding of historical views and materials. If the interpreter interprets Marx and Engels based on the former's own historical materials and perspectives, it is likely that the interpreter will suit the interpretation to their own needs. This very much explains the divergent understandings of the "Asiatic mode of production." We contend that study of the "Asiatic mode of production" needs to be based on historical documents rather than on subjective imagination or personal logic. However, we must distinguish between historical documents available to and those unavailable to Marx and Engels. We need to use the former in our interpretation of Marx and Engels. For the discussion whether the discourse of Marx and Engels conforms to different countries' real historical conditions, we must utilize both historical documents available to Marx and Engels and subsequently discovered documents, in our assessment of "real historical conditions." Detailed discussion on this issue will follow.

Principle two. The concept of the "Asian mode of production" of Marx and Engels is a historical concept, carrying different implications for different historical periods. Accordingly, the interpretation of the concept needs to consider different historical contexts as defined by Marx and Engels. Another reason why interpretations of the concept diverge is that certain scholars fail to consider the history of the concept's evolution. Some interpret the concept based on Marxist discourse of one historical period, while others, of another period. Reversely, some scholars utilize a large and incoherent medley of Marxist discourse and come to an unduly expanded interpretation of the concept in terms of both time and geography. They begin to include in their consideration a country (or region) or a certain development stage of a country originally not of the "Asiatic mode of production." This is seen in the book *Marx and the Third World* by Professor Umberto Melotti of the Milan Arts Academy in Italy. He mingled Marx and Engels' discourses of different times on the "Asiatic mode of production." On the surface, his discussion appears comprehensive and systematic or objective and fair. In reality, however, it is a fragmented and misguided interpretation. Professor Melotti's book discussed a total of 23 questions such as "the origin of the Asiatic mode of production," "Marx's theoretical source of the Asiatic mode of production," "basic characteristics of Asian society," "class structure of the Asian society," "differences among Asian society, ancient society, and feudal society," "unique cultural characteristics of Asian society," "types of Asian society," "what belongs to the 'Asian society' that Marx believed?," "Half-Asian Russian society," "long-term social stagnation due to the Asiatic mode of production," and "China—the most typical example of 'Asian society' in Marxist sense." According to Professor Melotti, almost all countries and regions in the world, with the exception of Western Europe and North America, are based on the "Asiatic mode of production." He classified China, Egypt, India, and Babylon as typical Asian societies; Persia and Byzantium as sub-Asian societies; Mongolia and Arab as quasi-Asian societies; Russia as a semi-Asian society; and Japan before the Meiji Restoration as a pseudo-Asian society.

Professor Melotti's view has a strong bourgeois ideological tendency. Theoretically, he called Marx and Engels' theory of five social forms "Mono-linear Theory," which he negated in favor of the "Multi-linear Theory" of social development. Professor Melotti over-emphasized the diversity of the historical development of each country, and negated any unity within such development, thus denying the objective regularity that is independent of human will. His attempt is to fundamentally undermine historical materialism. Politically, Melotti described China as a typical Asian society (Marx originally regarded India as a typical Asian society), and China's socialist system as the resurrection of the "Asiatic mode of production." He defamed the Chinese socialist system as a "bureaucratic collective system" which gives a political tint to his seemingly academic discussion of the "Asiatic mode of production." Therefore, I uphold two principles for the discussion of the Marxist concept of the "Asiatic mode of production." One, complete freedom of expression to all academic views and investigations. Two, denunciation of partisan politics put forth in disguise of anti-Marxism or anti-socialism.

Principle three. We need to correctly assess the relationship between Marx and Engels' thoughts and their assessments of these thoughts based on certain historical materials that do not conform to the actual development of Eastern society. As inquisitive scholars, Marx and Engels conducted in-depth research on Western philosophy, history, and economics, as well as on the development of Western history. They also researched deeply on ancient history and Eastern history, especially the history of India, China, and Russia, and produced their own unique insights. However, human as they were, Marx and Engels were neither omniscient nor free from historical limitations. The historical materials for their discussion of the Eastern society and especially Asian society were mostly writings of Western travelers, diplomats, missionaries, colonial officials, and some scholars from the 17th and 18th centuries. These materials were often fragmented and inaccurate. With no direct access to the reality of the Eastern society, Marx and Engels faced challenges in formulating completely accurate conclusions about the Eastern society. For instance, Marx and Engels thought that private land ownership did not exist in the East, that the Eastern society suffered from long-term stagnation, and that the Eastern rural commune and public ownership of land were foundations of the autocratic system, etc. These do not conform to the complete historical reality of Asia, especially that of China in history. In addition, Marx's generalization of certain characteristics of Eastern society does not have universal applicability. Some may be suitable only for Mesopotamia, some only for India, and some only for China. However, Marx and Engels offered no explicit indication on which of their characteristics were applicable for which part of the Eastern society. If we believe that the characteristics suitable only for certain countries and regions are also suitable for all countries in the East, we may have misunderstood and misapplied Marxist thoughts. In this case, we should adopt two principles. One, we need to interpret Marxism in accordance with the historical materials available to Marx and Engels. Two, we need to ascertain the authentic social conditions of the Eastern society and those elements in Marx and Engels' historical documents not in keeping with the reality of Eastern history. On this, more will follow.

Notes

1 *An Anthology of Marx and Engels* (Vol. 2). (2009). Beijing, China: People's Publishing House.
2 *An Anthology of Marx and Engels* (Vol. 7). (2009). Beijing, China: People's Publishing House.

2 Evolution of the concept of the "Asiatic mode of production"

This chapter explores the historical evolution of the concept of the "Asiatic mode of production" in works of Marx and Engels over four periods—before 1853, mid-to-late 1850s, the period represented by *Capital*, and the period after Morgan's publication of *Ancient Society*.

2.1 Before 1853

The German Ideology co-written by Marx and Engels in 1845 to 1846 was the first work marking the basic formation of historical materialism. In this work, the two authors presented their initial insights into social formation and its developmental laws. They analyzed social structure based on contradictions between productive forces and production relations and ascribed the development of human history to the development of production relations (forms of ownership). They said,

> The various stages of development in the division of labour are just so many different forms of ownership, i.e., the existing stage in the division of labour determines also the relations of individuals to one another with reference to the material, instrument, and product of labour.[1]

Here, the two authors expressed their rudimentary thought concerning social classification based on ownership forms as determined by productivity, and divided pre-capitalistic history into three forms of ownership: "tribal ownership," "ancient communal and State ownership," and "feudal or estate property."[2] We make the following proposals concerning these three forms of ownership:

First, the second and third forms of ownership mentioned by Marx and Engels are roughly and respectively equivalent to the slave society and feudal society in Western Europe, on which there is little scholarly controversy. Controversy exists over the first form of ownership. Regarding this form of ownership, Marx and Engels said:

> It corresponds to the undeveloped stage of production, at which a people lives by hunting and fishing, by the rearing of beasts or, in the highest stage,

> agriculture. In the latter case it presupposes a great mass of uncultivated stretches of land. The division of labour is at this stage still very elementary and is confined to a further extension of the natural division of labour existing in the family. The social structure is, therefore, limited to an extension of the family; patriarchal family chieftains, below them the members of the tribe, finally slaves. The slavery latent in the family only develops gradually with the increase of population, the growth of wants, and with the extension of external relations, both of war and of barter.[3]

Therefore, the "tribal ownership" has two main characteristics: (1) Productivity and division of labor were very underdeveloped. At that time, people lived by hunting and fishing, by the rearing of beasts or, in the highest stage, by agriculture. (2) The social structure is dominated by the patriarchal family chieftain, who governed members of society and slaves.

With regard to the "tribal ownership" proposed by Marx and Engels, there is considerable controversy among Chinese scholars. Some think that such ownership is the original commune system, since productivity and division of labor were still underdeveloped at that time. Others believe that the ownership was a confrontational social organization because slavery already existed. Both views may be simplistic and one-sided. We should examine and define the exact meaning of the concept of "tribal ownership" based on the formation and development of Marx and Engels' theory on societal classification.

The German Ideology was Marx and Engels' earliest work on ancient society and societal classification. Their study on social history at that time was limited to European society. Before this book, Marx had studied European history of more than 2,500 years, from the 6th century B.C. to the 1830s, especially the French Revolution which had a major impact on the modern history of the world, and the history of the United Kingdom, Germany, Sweden, Poland, and Venice. At that time, Marx and Engels were in their youth and did not yet begin their study on the history of Eastern society. They began their study on Asian society after the 1850s, and mainly studied the history of ancient Indian society. In the book *The German Ideology*, Marx and Engels' societal classification was formed before their study of Asian society. The book only manifested their understanding of the historical process of European society, which was not extremely convincing in terms of theorization and historical documentation. The "tribal ownership" mentioned in the book was equivalent to the clan commune ownership in primitive society in terms of economic structure, at a time when clan commune ownership was disintegrating and the slavery society began to appear. Marx and Engels did not yet distinguish between the clan commune and the village commune that emerged after the dissolution of the clan commune. "Tribal ownership" still represented a transition from the primitive society to the slave society. However, Marx and Engels were not consciously cognizant of this point as they had not yet formulated a comprehensive theory about primitive society. They still regarded this ownership as the first independent social form in history. At that time, Marx and Engels had neither discovered the unique characteristics that distinguished the West from the East, nor conceived the "Asiatic mode of production." Some scholars equate the "tribal ownership" in the book with the "Asiatic mode of production" as proposed by Marx in the *Preface to A Contribution to the Critique of Political Economy* in 1859. This view is not well-formulated.

Second, the three forms of ownership mentioned above existed before capitalism. They developed sequentially from the low to the high level, rather than coexisting simultaneously in different locations. Some Chinese scholars regard these three forms of ownership as three different types of ownership at the same stage of development, an idea untenable as judged by the narratives of Marx and Engels.

Third, Marx and Engels had realized that human history began with public ownership, moved on to private ownership, which then will be replaced by the public ownership of communism. Thus, the three forms of ownership prior to capitalism, plus the private ownership of capitalism, which will be replaced by the public ownership of the future communist society, give us five forms of ownership. With these five forms of ownership, come five social forms—society of tribal ownership, slave society, feudal society, capitalistic society, and communist society (socialism being its initial stage). These five social forms follow a low-to-high sequence in human history.

In short, when Marx and Engels first formulated their historical materialism, they were still incomplete in their theory of the "five social forms." In that theory, "tribal ownership" as the first form of society was not equivalent to the primitive society as they later proposed.

In *Wage Labour and Capital* written at the end of 1847 and published in April 1849, Marx first introduced his theory of social classification and evolution. He said:

> We thus see that the social relations within which individuals produce, the social relations of production, are altered, and transformed, with the change and development of the material means of production, of the forces of production. The relations of production in their totality constitute what is called the social relations, society, and, moreover, a society at a definite stage of historical development, a society with peculiar, distinctive characteristics. Ancient society, feudal society, and bourgeois (or capitalist) society, are such totalities of relations of production, each of which denotes a particular stage of development in the history of mankind.[4]

The three social formations of classical ancient society (referring to the slave society in Ancient Greece and Rome), the feudal society, and the capitalist society Marx discussed here, plus the social formation existing prior to the ancient society and the future communist social formation (socialism as its first stage), give us an ascending sequence of five social formations.

The Communist Manifesto, co-written by Marx and Engels between late 1847 and early 1848 and published in February 1848, debuted Marxism to the world. The two authors claim:

> Freeman and slave, patrician and plebeian, lord and serf, guild-master and journeyman, in a word, oppressor and oppressed, stood in constant opposition to one another, carried on an uninterrupted, now hidden, now open fight, a fight that each time ended, either in a revolutionary re-constitution of society at large, or in the common ruin of the contending classes.[5]

Marx and Engels had realized at that time that social hierarchy can be found almost everywhere in the earlier epochs of history. In Ancient Rome we had patricians, knights, plebeians, slaves; in the Middle Ages: feudal lords, vassals, guild-masters, journeymen, apprentices, and serfs.

> The modern bourgeois society that has sprouted from the ruins of feudal society has not done away with class antagonisms. It has but established new classes, new conditions of oppression, and new forms of struggle in place of the old ones.
>
> Our epoch, the epoch of the bourgeoisie, possesses, however, this distinctive feature: it has simplified the class antagonisms. Society as a whole is more and more splitting up into two great hostile camps, into two great classes directly facing each other: Bourgeoisie and Proletariat.[6]

These discussions by Marx and Engels indicate the class status of the slave society, feudal society, and capitalist society. As its goal, the *Manifesto* is to reveal that capitalism will inevitably be replaced by future communism. Here, Marx and Engels regarded the slave society, feudal society, capitalist society, and communist society as four social formations in an ascending sequence. If we add in the social formation before the slave society, there would be a sequence of exactly five social forms.

In summary, in the mid and late 1940s, Marx and Engels proposed the theory of five social forms based on their study of European history. However, this theory was not yet fully mature and was in need of further improvement.

In the early 1950s, Marx and Engels began to study problems of the oriental society and extended their vision from the West to the East. This was due to two reasons. First, after the failure of the European Revolution in 1848–1849, Marx and Engels placed their hopes on the national liberation movement in Eastern countries oppressed by European capitalism. At that time, the Taiping Heavenly Kingdom Movement led by Hong Xiuquan broke out in China. This movement revealed that China was on the eve of a great transformation. Marx and Engels believed that the national liberation movement in the East would impact Europe and accelerate the outbreak of a new revolution there. Marx wrote in the article "Revolution in China and in Europe" in 1853:

> Under these circumstances, as the greater part of the regular commercial circle has already been run through by British trade, it may safely be augured that the Chinese revolution will throw the spark into the overloaded mine of the present industrial system and cause the explosion of the long-prepared general crisis, which, spreading abroad, will be closely followed by political revolutions on the Continent. It would be a curious spectacle, that of China sending disorder into the Western World while the Western Powers, by English, French and American war-steamers, are conveying "order" to Shanghai, Nanking and the mouths of the Great Canal.[7]

Second, in 1853, the British Parliament had a discussion on extending the East India Company's Charter, which drew Marx's great concern and attention. To express his views on this discussion and to facilitate his study on the Indian issue, Marx put forward in his article "The Future Results of British Rule in India" written on July 22, 1853, the concept of "Asiatic society" for the first time and differentiated this concept from "Western society." Marx and Engels believed that the "Asiatic society," as opposed to the "Western society," mainly had the following characteristics:

First, the absence of private landed property is indeed key to understanding the East. On June 2, 1853, in a letter to Engels, based on François Bernier's *Travels in the Mogul Empire*, Marx said, "Bernier rightly sees all the manifestations of the East—he mentions Turkey, Persia and Hindustan—as having a common basis, namely the *absence of private landed property*. This is the real clef, even to the eastern heaven."[8] In a reply to Marx on June 6, Engels agreed: "The absence of landed property is indeed the key to the whole of the East. Therein lies its political and religious history."

Engels attributed the absence of private land ownership to the geography of these countries. He said:

> But how to explain the fact that oriental never reached the stage of landed property, not even the feudal kind? This is, I think, largely due to the climate, combined with the nature of the land, more especially the great stretches of desert extending from the Sahara right across Arabia, Persia, India and Tartary to the highest of the Asiatic uplands. Here artificial irrigation is the first prerequisite for agriculture, and this is the responsibility either of the communes, the provinces or the central government.[9]

In the article "The British Rule in India" written on June 10, Marx incorporated the idea of Engels, but held a lightly different view. Apart from the reason that Engels gave for the absence of private land ownership in the East—geography—Marx added another important reason—low productivity. Marx said:

> This prime necessity of an economical and common use of water, which, in the Occident, drove private enterprise to voluntary association, as in Flanders and Italy, necessitated, in the Orient where civilization was too low and the

> territorial extent too vast to call into life voluntary association, the interference of the centralizing power of Government.[10]

Marx ascribed "different levels of civilization" or of productivity as the main reason behind different land ownerships between the East and the West. This view, ironically, both proposed the particularity of the Eastern society and sowed the seed for its negation. In other words, the historical-materialistic view of productivity as the ultimate determinant of social progress somewhat confutes the particularity of the Eastern society. It is worthy of note that in their discussion of the Eastern society, Marx and Engels mentioned India but not China. This indicates that, they, unlike Umberto Melotti, believed that India rather than China typified the "Asiatic mode of production."

Marx and Engels' discourse on the non-existence of private landed property in Asia is mainly based on the description and investigation of land issues of the Mogul Empire in India by Western writers. In his book *Travels in the Mogul Empire*, the French physician, traveler, and writer François Bernier of the 17th century said:

> The Great Mogol constitutes himself heir of all the Omrahs, or lords, and likewise of the Mansebdars, or inferior lords, who are in his pay; and, what is of the utmost importance, that he is proprietor of every acre of land in the kingdom … . The courtiers are often not even descendants of Omrahs, because, the King being heir of all their possessions, no family can long maintain its distinction.

He continued:

> The King, as proprietor of the land, makes over a certain quantity to military men, as an equivalent for their pay; and this grant is called jah-ghir, or, as in Turkey, timar … Similar grants are made to governors, in lieu of their salary.[11]

Western scholars' understanding of the Eastern land system in the 18th century inherited those of the writers in the 17th century. For example, Montesquieu said in the book *The Spirit of the Laws*: "Of all despotic governments there is none that labours more under its own weight than that wherein the prince declares himself proprietor of all the lands, and heir to all his subjects. Hence the neglect of agriculture arises."[12] This obviously follows Bernier's point of view. In *An Inquiry into the Nature and Causes of the Wealth of Nations*, British classical economist Adam Smith discussed the issue of state ownership of land in China, India, Egypt, and other Eastern countries. Smith said:

> The sovereigns of China, of ancient Egypt, and of the different nations into which Indostan has at different times been divided, have derived the whole, or by far the most considerable part, of revenue from some sort of land tax

> or land rent … . In China, the principal revenue of the sovereign consists in a part of the produce of all lands of the empire. This tenth part…[13]

The combination of rent and tax that Adam Smith mentioned is actually an important argument of the subsequent theory of the state ownership of land in the East.

The preceding arguments of the western writers on the non-existence of private property in land in eastern countries do not accord with the history of the East. Indeed, in some eastern countries, such as India, the common ownership of land by village communities had long been in existence in various areas and the transformation from the common ownership of land to private property was extremely slow. By time of the Mogul Empire, that transformation was still in process. In the actual course of history, however, private land ownership dated back to the Indian Harappan Civilization (2700–1500 B.C.). A variety of Buddhism literature of the 6th to 4th centuries B.C. also recorded the private property in land.[14] In China, the common ownership of the land prevailed in the Xia, Shang, and Zhou Dynasties. After Shang Yang's reforms, landlord land ownership took hold from the Qin and Han Dynasties.

In fact, with their deepened understanding of the Eastern land system, Marx and Engels gradually changed their views on the "non-existence of the private landed property in the East." In his preparatory materials for *Anti-Dühring*, Engels said: "All civilised peoples begin with the common ownership of the land. It is abolished, negated, and after a longer or shorter series of intermediate stages is transformed into private property."[15] In *Anti-Dühring* written in 1876 to 1878, Engels regarded the transformation from the common ownership of land to private property in land and to a higher form of common ownership as the common evolution of all forms of land ownership of civilized peoples. He said:

> All civilised peoples begin with the common ownership of the land. With all peoples who have passed a certain primitive stage, this common ownership becomes in the course of the development of agriculture a fetter on production. It is abolished, negated, and after a longer or shorter series of intermediate stages is transformed into private property. But at a higher stage of agricultural development, brought about by private property in land itself, private property conversely becomes a fetter on production, as is the case today both with small and large land ownership. The demand that it, too, should be negated, that it should once again be transformed into common property, necessarily arises. But this demand does not mean the restoration of the aboriginal common ownership, but the institution of a far higher and more developed form of possession in common.[16]

We know that Engels had read all the manuscripts of *Anti-Dühring* to Marx before they saw print. Marx apparently agreed with Engels' thoughts.

In his *Abstract of Maxim Kovalevsky's Communal Landownership, and the Causes, Course and Consequences of Its Disintegration* (Vol. 1, Moscow, 1879) written in 1879 and 1880, Marx excerpted Kovalevsky's narration of the five stages of the Indian land system, from common ownership to private property: (1) Initially, the clan commune which featured land common ownership and collective cultivation was implemented. (2) The clan communes were divided into family communes based on clan branches, thus ending the indivisibility of land ownership and the collective cultivation of land. (3) Land ownership based on inheritance, which leads to inequitable land ownership. (4) Inequitable land ownership based not on one's proximity with the clan chieftain, but on tillage-determined actual occupation of the land. (5) Periodical reallocation of commune land, by long or short terms. At first, houses (and their adjacent land), cultivated land, and grassland were equally reallocated. Then the land adjacent to the houses (including the land in the vicinity of the residence) was turned into private property, as then were the cultivated land and grassland. The collective family was also increasingly simplified into a modern individual family.[17] Marx's abstracts and comments seem to give the conclusion that Marx basically agreed with Kovalevsky's argument. This shows that Marx thought over the land system in India from the duality of common ownership and private property and the transition from the former to the latter. In the late 1870s, Marx no longer insisted on the idea of the non-existence of private landed property in India.

Second, the whole country was divided into many separate and self-sufficient village communes with the combination of agricultural and handicraft industries, which furnished a solid foundation for the Eastern despotism and long-term stagnation. Marx said:

> These two circumstances – the Hindoo, on the one hand, leaving, like all Oriental peoples, to the Central Government the care of the great public works, the prime condition of his agriculture and commerce, dispersed, on the other hand, over the surface of the country, and agglomerated in small centers by the domestic union of agricultural and manufacturing pursuits – these two circumstances had brought about, since the remotest times, a social system of particular features – the so-called *village system* [emphasis added], which gave to each of these small unions their independent organization and distinct life.

These villages seldom had contact with each other and remained isolated, looking as if atoms of the same appearance but with no association. "Those family-communities were based on domestic industry, in that peculiar combination of hand-weaving, hands-spinning and hand-tilling agriculture which gave them self-supporting power."[18] In a letter to Engels on June 14, 1853, Marx portrayed the specific conditions of the Indian village communities and denoted that they constituted a solid basis for the Indian despotism and long-term stagnation. He said:

> In some of these communities the lands of the village were cultivated in common, in most of them each occupant tills his own field. Within the same, slavery and the caste system. Waste lands for common pasture. Home-weaving and spinning by wives and daughters. These idyllic republics, of which only

> the *village boundaries are jealously guarded* against neighbouring villages, continue to exist in well-nigh perfect form in the North Western parts of India only recently occupied by the English. No more solid basis for Asiatic despotism and stagnation is, I think, conceivable.[19]

The statement that the village community and the common ownership of the land are the basis of the Eastern despotism is not in line with the true history of the East. During the existence of the village community system and the common ownership of the land in the Western Zhou Dynasty, the centralized monarchy was not consolidated, and the legacy of the primitive democracy still somewhat existed. The absolute monarchy, which consolidated from the Qin and Han Dynasties, coincided with the collapse of the village commune and private land's replacement of public land. The history of the political system of China's feudal society shows that the state apparatus of the centralized autocratic system based on the private property of landlords and smallholders is more consolidated and powerful than that of the despotism based on the village commune and the common ownership of land.

Third, manual irrigation in agriculture was of paramount importance. The construction and management of public water conservancy projects and traffic roads were in the centralized government's charge. Marx pointed out: "There have been in Asia, generally, from immemorial times, but three departments of Government; that of Finance, or the plunder of the interior; that of War, or the plunder of the exterior; and, finally, the department of Public Works." In Egypt, India, Mesopotamia, Persia, or other areas, people used flooding river water to fertilize their fields and fill the irrigation ditches. "Hence an economical function devolved upon all Asiatic Governments, the function of providing public works. This artificial fertilization of the soil, dependent on a Central Government, and immediately decaying with the neglect of irrigation and drainage."[20] The British inherited the departments of Finance and War from their predecessors in East India but completely ignored the department of Public Works. Then agriculture in India decayed, where the crop depended on the government, just like Europe where the crop depended on the weather.

Fourth, the Asian society had been stagnant for a long time and lacked an inherent impetus for development. Only the invasion by Western capitalism could shake its foundation and incite a real social revolution in Asia. Marx believed that India's village community had no significance and did not promote social progress. From time immemorial to the 1810s, the social structure and condition in India had not changed despite political upheavals there. In this case, only the invasion from Western capitalism can break this stagnation and accelerate the development of the Asian society. On the one hand, Marx expressed great indignation at the brutal crimes of British colonialism's aggression and plunders in India and severely condemned them. On the other hand, he affirmed that humans cannot complete their historical missions without fundamental revolutions in the Asian societies. Therefore, no matter how many crimes the British committed in India, they instigated the social revolution and served as an unintended tool for historical progression. Britain had to fulfill its dual missions in India: One is destruction—the elimination of the old Asian-style society; the other is reconstruction—laying of a material foundation for the Western-style society in Asia.

The four characteristics of Asian society by Marx and Engels indicate their belief that the Asian society was an ancient regional social form completely different and independent from the Western European society before the invasion by Western capitalism in the 18th and 19th centuries. On the one hand, Marx and Engels just expanded their horizons from Europe to Asia and the historical materials under their possession were not yet sufficient; on the other, they were affected by the incomplete and inaccurate historical data provided by Western writers, thus failing to place Asia's history properly into the evolutionary sequence of the five social formations that they proposed in the mid to late 1840s based on European history. Their proposal of the "five social formations" theory based only on European history was not yet fully mature; when they just started to study the Asian society, they saw more differences than similarities between Asia and the Western European society, a fact largely in line with the general development of human cognition. Be that as it may, this must be the theoretical flaw in their social formation theory during that period. If only based on Marx and Engels' discussion of the characteristics of the Asian society in the early 1850s, it is true that the Asian society can be seen as an ancient regional social form completely different from the Western European society, just as what Umberto Melotti claimed in *Marx and the Third World.* However, Marx and Engels changed their views on the Asian society after further study of world history. They gradually gave up the conception of Asian society as an unaltered, independent, and regional social formation.

2.2 Mid to late 1850s

From 1857 to 1859, based on his study of the Asian society in the early 1850s, Marx further researched and compared the Asian and European societies and enriched his theory of the successive replacement of the five social formations which he proposed in the mid to late 1840s.

His works in this period include "Pre-Capitalist Economic Formations" seen in *Economic Manuscripts of 1857–1858*, *Introduction to A Contribution to the Critique of Political Economy*, and *Preface to A Contribution to the Critique of Political Economy*. Major contents of these works are summarized below.

2.2.1 About the formations of primitive ownership

In the chapter "Pre-Capitalist Economic Formations," Marx divided primitive ownership into three forms—the Asiatic form, the classical ancient form, and the Germanic form. Compared with capitalist production modes, these three forms of ownership share commonalities, such as the combination of objective conditions of laborers and of labor, and individuals' varied dependence on the community. However, they differ from each other in two aspects:

First, land ownership and management are different.

In Asia, there is no private land ownership.

> Where property exists *only* as communal property, … the individual member as such is only the *possessor* of a particular part of it, hereditary or not, for any fraction of property belongs to no member for himself, but only as the direct part of the community, consequently as someone in direct unity with the community and not as distinct from it. The individual is therefore only a possessor. What exists is only *communal* property and *private possession*.[21]

The land in Asia belongs to the commune or a consortium of communes. Commune members had use but no ownership of the land. Under this form of land ownership, land was managed differently in different locations and at different times, which may be summarized in two major ways. One, the individual, together with the family, worked on their assigned land. Two, under the regulation of the commune or a larger association of the communes, the laborer worked on the land and formed their institutions, as seen in Mexico and especially in Peru, among the ancient Celts, and among some tribes of India.

In classical ancient ownership, land was divided into common land and private land. "Common land—as state property, ager publicus—is here separate from private property."

> In antiquity (Romans as the classic example, the thing in its purest and most clearly marked form), there is a contradictory form of state landed property and private landed property, so that the latter is mediated through the former, or the former exists only in this double form.[22]

That is to say, in the classical ancient ownership, private ownership of land had emerged, and there was a confrontation between private land ownership and public land ownership; private landed property is mediated through the state landed property. Only as a member of the commune can individuals get a piece of land. Families cultivated their private land and the produce was private; the commune members cultivated the common land, and the produce was returned to the commune.

In the Germanic form of ownership, although there are also common and private lands, the common land was different from that in the classical ancient form of ownership. The common land does not represent a special economy of the country coexisting with the private land, but a communal accessory of the private land. Common land was not dominant and did not exist independently. As Marx said,

> Individual landed property does not here appear as a contradictory form of communal landed property, nor as mediated by the community, but the other way around. The community exists only in the mutual relation of the individual landowners as such. Communal property as such appears only as a communal accessory to the individual kin settlements and land appropriations.

Common land served as a means of production in some hunting grounds, common pastures, or woodlands. Meanwhile, it was used by individual households and needed not to be operated by commune members. "At bottom, every individual household contains an entire economy, forming as it does an independent centre of production (manufacture merely the domestic subsidiary labor of the women, etc.)."[23]

So what are the reasons for these different forms of land ownership? Marx offered his explanation. He pointed out that in whatever form—common ownership, or the dual form of state ownership and private ownership, or communal property as a supplement to private property—

> [t]hese different forms of relationship of communal tribal members to the tribal land—to the earth upon which it has settled—depend partly on the natural character [Naturanlagen] of the tribe, partly on the economic conditions in which the tribe really exercises its ownership of the land—i.e., appropriates its fruits by means of labor. And this in turn will depend on the climate, the physical properties of the soil, the physically conditioned mode of its utilization, the relationships to hostile or neighboring tribes, and such modification as are introduced by migrations, historical events, etc.[24]

Marx offered four reasons to explain the different forms of land ownership: (1) Different natural conditions such as climate and the physical properties of the soil; (2) different levels of productivity or economic conditions; (3) relationships to hostile or neighboring tribes; and (4) the influence of migrations and other historical events.

Second, the individual's dependence on the community (the commune), and the social structures are different.

The individual's dependence on the community and social structures in the Asiatic commune have the following characteristics: (1) The community is a very strong commune on which the individual has the strongest dependence. The community is an entity, while the individual is merely an accessory to or a natural part of the entity. Each individual, only as a part or member of the community can regard themselves as the owner or possessor. (2) Small communes combined to form the consortium, which in the form of state or dictatorship ruled over the individual communes. The consortium is the higher and sole owner of land, depriving the individual members of their land. In other words, property

> appears to be mediated by means of a grant from the total unity to the individual through the intermediary of the particular community. The despot here appears as the father of all the numerous lesser communities, thus realizing the common unity of all.[25]

The despot or their government usurped and exploited the surplus labor of the individual without compensation. (3) Water conservancy and irrigation facilities and important means of transportation were managed by the despotic government in a unified manner. Marx said,

> The communal conditions for real appropriation through labor, such as *irrigation systems* (very important among the Asian peoples), means of communication, etc., will then appear as the work of the higher unity—the despotic government which is poised above the lesser communities.[26]

(4) Members of the commune took the village as their domicile, took land as the foundation, as the city was underdeveloped. Cities in the proper sense arose by the side of these villages only where the location was particularly favorable to external trade, or where the head of the state and their satraps exchanged their revenue (the surplus product) against labor, which they expended as labor funds. There are no producing activities in cities, "the large city, properly speaking, must be regarded merely as a princely camp, superimposed on the real economic structure."[27] (5) The economic form was of the self-sufficient natural type combining agriculture and handicraft industry, characterized by protracted stagnation, small, slow changes, and the longest time to maintain. Marx said,

> The Asiatic form necessarily survives the longest and most stubbornly. This is due to the fundamental principle on which it is based—that is, that the individual does not become independent of the community; that the circle of production is self-sustaining, unity of agriculture and craft manufacture, etc.[28]

He added,

> The more traditional the mode of production itself, i.e., the more the real process of appropriation remains the same, the more unchanging will the ancient forms of property be and therefore also the community as a whole. (Note that the traditional mode persists for a long time in agriculture and even longer in the oriental combination of agriculture and manufacture.)[29]

In terms of the individual's dependence on the community and social structure in the ancient commune, we find the following characteristics: (1) The small peasant cultivators and the consortium of communes are interdependent. Members of the commune or consortium of communes guarantee each other's existence. On the one hand, the foundation of the commune is its members as independent, small peasant cultivators. If the peasants lose their plot of land, the communes will decay. Therefore, the commune must guarantee that independent farmers own their plot of land. On the other hand, farmers can own small pieces of land exactly due to the existence of communes. The farmers must work to cultivate common land and contribute surplus labor to the commune to guarantee its existence. (2) The farmers who constitute the commune are equal to each other. Members of the commune have the right to occupy a small piece of land as an objective condition for labor, but they must personally participate in labor in order to continue to maintain this small piece of land. If the equal relationship between the farmers who constitute the commune is destroyed, the commune will decay. (3) Residents regard cities as foundation and residential centers, and the cultivated land serves as the territory of the city. Urban communes are organized on military lines, as a warlike or military force. Its mission is to protect the independence of the commune so that it will not be destroyed or annexed by other communes, or to plunder the land property of other communes in order to enhance the objective conditions of its existence, leading to wars between communes. (4) The commune is a self-sufficient economy. The main economic sectors are: small-scale agriculture producing for immediate consumption; manufacture as the domestic subsidiary, labor of wives and daughters (spinning and weaving), and some additional independent industries such as those of handicraftsmen.

In terms of the individual's dependence on the community and social structure in the Germanic commune, we find the following characteristics: (1) The community is loose. It exists not as an independent entity but embedded in other collective groups and activities. The members of the commune are rarely dependent on the community. Marx said,

> In the Germanic form, the agriculturalist is not a citizen—i.e., not an inhabitant of cities—but its foundation is the isolated, independent family settlement, guaranteed by means of its association with other such settlements by men of the same tribe, and their occasional assembly for purposes of war, religion, the settlement of legal disputes, etc., which establishes their mutual surety.[30]

(2) Members of the commune lived neither in the rural nor in the urban area. All these families live in the forest, far away from each other. They usually have no connection, and only come into contact when they have an assembly. As Marx said: "In the Germanic world, the individual home, which itself appears merely as a point in the land belonging to it, there is no concentration of a multiplicity of proprietors, but the family as an independent unit."[31] (3) The common land of the community has a separate economic existence, communally used by every individual proprietor as hunting grounds and pastures. These individuals differ from the representatives of the state as in ancient communes. That is to say, this common land "is genuinely the common property of the individual owners, and not of the union of owners, possessing an existence of its own in the city, distinct from that of the individual members."[32] Therefore, the fruits of labor of the individual belong to themselves, and there is no need to serve or pay tax to any other person or entity, because there is no such person or entity among the Germans.

In addition to analyzing the differences between the three primitive forms of ownership, Marx compared them with the capitalist mode of production, revealing the commonality shared among the former but not present in capitalism. Their shared commonality may be summarized as follows: (1) The objective conditions of labor are not the result but the premise of labor. Individuals simply regard the objective conditions of labor as their own. The objective conditions of such labor are not the product of labor but are directly provided by nature. (2) An individual belongs to a certain community and is a member of this community. Once the individual leaves this community, he/she cannot exist and there is no personal property. (3) The laborer and the objective conditions of labor are directly combined. The separation of laborers and the objective conditions of labor have not yet appeared. (4) The economic form is a self-sufficient natural economy. The purpose of laborers' production is to create use value, rather than exchange value.

The reason why Marx investigated three primitive forms of ownership in detail is to explain the premises of capitalism. There are two premises for capitalism: (1) Workers are separated and free from the objective conditions; (2) free workers can be used in exchange for money. Marx said:

> One of the prerequisites of wage labor, and one of the historic conditions for capital, is free labor and the exchange of free labor against money, in order to reproduce money and to convert it into values, in order to be consumed by money, not as use value for enjoyment, but as use value for money. Another prerequisite is the separation of free labor from the objective conditions of its realization—from the means and material of labor. This means above all that the workers must be separated from the land, which functions as his natural laboratory. This means the dissolution both of free petty landownership and of communal landed property, based on the oriental commune.

The three primitive forms of land ownership do not possess the two premises for capitalism. Only the dissolution of the three primitive forms of land ownership and the dissolution of smallholdings (created after the dissolution of the three primitive forms of land ownership) are the prerequisites of capitalism.

2.2.2 The transition from the "primitive form" to the "derived form"

Marx believed that although the Asiatic, classical ancient, and the Germanic forms of ownership are primitive, they are no longer the most primitive but often modified forms of ownership. At that time, Marx had not discovered the most primitive form of ownership. He pointed out that the community, "though it is here not merely a de facto product of history, but one of which men are conscious as such, has therefore had an origin." Marx made it clearer in the *Third Draft of Letter To Vera Zasulich* in 1881,

> The agricultural commune (i.e., Asiatic commune, ancient classical commune, and Germanic commune) is the last stage of the primary social form. It is also a transition from the primary form to the secondary one, or from a society based on public ownership to a society based on private ownership. It is evident that the secondary form includes a series of societies based on slavery and serfdom.

That is to say, after the dissolution of the primitive form of ownership, a series of social forms such as slavery and serfdom (feudal society) will in turn emerge. Marx's statement shows that the Asiatic commune, the classical ancient commune, and Germanic commune are all final stages of the primitive society, a transition from the primitive society to the next form of society, or from the public ownership society to the private ownership society, from a classless society to a class society. This is the most scientific expression of the role of the three communes in the social development. Marx had such thoughts in late 1850s, though not yet expressed as precisely as above.

It's necessary to clarify Marx's following statement in the chapter "Forms Preceding Capitalist Production":

> If man himself is captured together with the land as an organic appendage of it, he is captured as one of the conditions of production, and this is the origin of slavery and serfdom, which soon debase and modify the original forms of all communities, and then themselves become their basis. The simple structure is thereby negatively determined.[33]

According to Marx's words, some people believe that the slave society and the feudal society appear not successively in history but rather simultaneously in different locations. After the dissolution of the primitive society, both a slave society and a feudal society are equally likely to be formed. Some people even argue the possibility that feudal society might precede slave society, as a way to negate Marx's theory that the five social forms represent a predetermined ascending sequence. This view misinterprets Marx. In a letter to Marx on December 22, 1882, Engels said: "It is certain that serfdom and bondage are not a peculiarly medieval-feudal form, we find them everywhere or nearly everywhere where conquerors have the land cultivated for them by the old inhabitants—e.g., very early in Thessaly."[34] This letter clearly shows that the serfdom described in Marx's above passage differs from that described in *Marx–Zasulich Correspondence*. The bondage mentioned in the *Correspondence* is a social form in a "series of social forms" (i.e., a feudal society) based on the serfdom in the Middle Ages in Europe. But the first one as quoted above (serfdom) refers to the primitive serfdom after foreign conquest of the tribal community. It is the predecessor of the medieval serfdom in Europe rather than of European medieval feudalism or European medieval serfdom based on the feudal society. Slavery is not a sufficient indication of the formation of the slave society. Likewise, serfdom is no sufficient indication of the formation of the feudal society. In place of the original commune after its dissolution, slavery, serfdom, or both, and sometimes even a wage labor system might emerge. However, at the level of productivity capable by the primitive society, only a slave society but neither a feudal society nor a capitalist society can emerge. Generally, a feudal society emerges only at a productivity level above that of the slave society and of course above that of the primitive society as well. Therefore, slave society precedes feudal society either in the logical sequence of history or based on the historical facts of most civilized countries in the world. The slave society and the feudal society are not two spatially juxtaposed social forms coexisting in different locations after dissolution of the primitive society. Just as the daughter cannot precede the mother, so the feudal society cannot precede the slave society.

Then, what dissolves the primitive form of ownership and causes its transformation to the derivative form? Marx's discussion of the issue in the chapter "Forms Preceding Capitalist Production" may be summarized as the following four points:

First, population increases and war conquests due to immigration would inevitably lead to slavery. As mentioned above, the laborer regards the objective conditions of labor as his or her own possession. As a premise for the existence of the primitive form of ownership, the individual belongs as a member to a certain community. But, "these conditions change," for instance,

> where each individual is supposed to possess a certain amount of land, the increase in population already presents a problem. If it is to be coped with, colonisation and with its wars of conquest have to be undertaken. Hence slaves, etc., also e.g. the enlargement of the ager publicus, and hence more patricians, who represent the community, etc.[35]

Second, due to increasing productivity and new labor division and methods, corresponding changes occur in relations of production.

> In the act of reproduction itself are changed not only the objective conditions—e.g. village becomes city, the wilderness becomes cultivated clearings, etc.—but also the producers, who transform themselves in that they evolve new qualities from within themselves, develop through production new powers and new ideas, new modes of intercourse, new needs, and new speech.[36]

Third, private ownership within the primitive form of ownership is the most important reason for its collapse. When discussing the classical ancient community, Marx said:

> Where the members of the community have already developed a separate entity as private proprietors from their collective entity as an urban community and owners of the urban territory, conditions already arise in which the individual may lose his property, i.e. the dual relationship which makes him both a citizen with equal status, belonging to the community, and a proprietor.[37]

The individual loses his status as a member of the community because of losing personal property, causing the inevitable collapse of the community.

Fourth, the commune members' hate of labor is another important reason for the collapse of the communes and the emergence of slavery. This hate makes it necessary to coerce slaves into work, leading to wars for more slaves. Coupled with the emergence of division of labor and exchanges, debts, etc., the gap between poor and rich exacerbates within the commune. The rich rise to become slave owners, and the poor degenerates into slaves, prompting the collapse of the commune.

2.2.3 Evolution of social forms and classification of social stages

Marx investigated both the static and dynamic perspectives for this topic.

From a static perspective, Marx juxtaposed the three primitive land ownerships. They are all transitions from the primitive form to the derivative form and belong to the same stage of social development. Some Chinese scholars argue that the three primitive land ownerships represent a chronological sequence—the Asiatic land ownership and then the classical ancient land ownership and then the Germanic land ownership. This viewpoint is not in line with Marx's original intention.

From a dynamic perspective (i.e., the transition from "primitive form" to "derivative form"), Marx believes that the "derivative forms" (as derived from the "primitive forms" of land ownership) represent a low-to-high sequence manifested at different stages of development. The production modes of Asia, Ancient Greece and Rome, and feudalism, mentioned by Marx in his *Preface to A Contribution to the Critique of Political Economy*, are respectively the "derivative forms" of "primitive forms" of the Asian, classical ancient, and Germanic forms of ownership.

In the mid-1840s, Marx formed the following two ideas. First, public ownership existed in the early stage of human society, and later transitioned to private ownership. Second, individuals' dependence on the community was stronger in the early stage of human society but weakened later.

Land ownership in Asia was public. Individuals held tenure but no ownership of land. Individuals strongly depended on the community. The community was secure in a protracted stagnation, with minimal changes in the transition from the "primitive form" to the "derivative form," wherein no derivative form was produced. Therefore, in some works such as *Preface to A Contribution to the Critique of Political Economy*, Marx regarded the "Asiatic" land ownership and "Asiatic mode of production" as the first social form in human history, and positioned it as the first stage of historical evolution.

The classical ancient ownership juxtaposes public and private ownerships. Individuals are less dependent on the community. The slave society of Ancient Greece and Rome was derived from this form of land ownership. Therefore, in works such as *Preface to A Contribution to the Critique of Political Economy*, Marx used the term "classical ancient history," "classical ancient society," or "ancient society" to designate the Western European slavery and considered it the second social form or stage in human history.

Germanic land ownership was private, and was the foundation of land ownership. Public land was supplementary to private land, and the community was loose, on which the individuals' dependence was weak. The serfdom-based feudal society derived directly from the Western Roman Empire, which conquered the slave society in history. Therefore, in works such as *Preface to A Contribution to the Critique of Political Economy*, Marx regarded "the Germanic history" or "the Germanic era" as the third social form or stage in human history.

In his 1895 *Preface to A Contribution to the Critique of Political Economy*, Marx generalized his theory of social forms and replacement, which was initially presented in the chapter "Forms Preceding Capitalist Production" in *Economic Manuscripts of 1857–1858*. In this preface, Marx regards production methods of Asia, Ancient Greece and Rome, and feudalism as different social forms in a low-to-high sequence rather than different ownerships coexisting at the same social stage.

Some people do not distinguish Marx's static investigation from the dynamic one and the "primitive form" of ownership from the "derivative form" of ownership. Therefore, Marx's three primitive ownerships, viewed as parallel in the static perspective, are mistaken for the three "derivative forms" of ownership, viewed as successive in the dynamic perspective. In other words, the three sequential "derivative forms" are mistaken for the three parallel "primitive forms." This undoubtedly and untenably denies the Marxian theory that the five social forms represent a low-to-high sequence.

In "Forms Preceding Capitalist Production," Marx said:

> Ancient classical history is the history of cities, but cities based on landed property and agriculture; Asiatic history is a kind of indifferent unity of town and country (the really large cities must be regarded here merely as royal camps, as an artificial excrescence on the actual economic structure); the Middle Ages (Germanic period) begins with the land as the locus of history, whose further development then proceeds through the contradiction between town and country; modern [history] is the urbanisation of the countryside, not, as in ancient times, the ruralisation of the city.[38]

Based on the discrepancy between the sequence seen here and that seen in *Preface to A Contribution to the Critique of Political Economy*, some scholars in China argue that the Asiatic mode of production, the slavery of Ancient Greece and Rome, and the feudalism of the Middle Ages are three parallel social forms coexisting in space, and that is why Marx does not put them in a consistent order. As such, these scholars negate the successive sequence of the five social forms. This argument is not tenable. Indeed, in *Preface to A Contribution to the Critique of Political Economy*, Marx puts the "Asiatic mode of production" in the first stage of historical development and the production method of Ancient Greece and Rome in the second stage; while in "Forms Preceding Capitalist Production," he puts "classical ancient history" (the history of Ancient Greece and Rome) before "Asian history." On the surface, it seems that Marx believes that the order is unimportant. However, a closer look reveals that the orders in the two books are given from different perspectives. *Preface to A Contribution to the Critique of Political Economy* is arranged in the order of social evolution, but the passage in "Forms Preceding Capitalist Production" addresses the different development levels or statuses of different cities and villages. It is obviously wrong to conclude that the sequence between the Asian mode of production and production mode of Ancient Greece and Rome can be arbitrarily reversed.

It should be especially noted that in some works, Marx used "ancient" or "classical ancient" as the name for the Ancient Greek and Roman slave society.

However, we should not conclude that this remains the case in all Marxian works. In the fields of history and philosophy, references to the term "ancient" or "classical ancient" differ not only among different scholars but also among different works of the same scholar at different times or even between different paragraphs within the same work.

Historians generally divide the history of Ancient Greece into five parts. In *World History*, edited by Wu Yuqin and Qi Shirong, the five parts are: (1) The Aegean civilization or the Crete Mycenaean civilization period (20th – 12th century B.C.); (2) the Homer period (11th–9th century B.C.); (3) the archaic period (8th–6th century B.C.); (4) the classical period (5th–4th century B.C.); (5) Macedonia's reign period (late 4th century B.C. to mid 2nd century B.C.).[39]Considering "classical ancient" as a specific stage in Ancient Greek history is a narrow understanding or definition of it. In addition, there is a generalized "classical ancient," which refers to the Ancient Greek and Roman civilizations. Zhu Longhua gives a good explanation in *World History-The Ancient Part*:

> In the history of Greek culture, the 5th century B.C. is called High Classic, and the next century is called Late Classic. Sometimes, the centuries are named as proper nouns "Five Century Five" and "Century Four" (without the suffix "B.C."). Strictly speaking, High Classic begins with the Marathon campaign, while Late Classic ends in the year 330, which gives not exactly an entire century. In addition, the classical period, composed of the two centuries, is a specific stage in the history of Greek culture, marking the prosperity and maturity of Greek civilization. To distinguish it from the prior simple ancient period (the "archaic period" in the above-mentioned stages—author) and the next Hellenistic period (general equivalent to the "Macedonia's reign period" in the above-mentioned stages—author), a narrow definition is used for the classical period. The reason is that we often regard the entire Ancient Greek civilization (even including Roman civilization) as classical civilization in world history. And the Greco-Roman period is also called the classical period or the classical world, which is a broad definition of the classical period. Based on the distinction between the above narrow and broad definitions, we begin to appreciate the classical peak in the 5th century B.C. as the most representative and essential period.[40]

Since "classical antiquity in a broad sense" refers to a rather long historical period, covering all phases of Ancient Greek and Roman civilization, the terms "ancient" or "classical ancient" used in different works or different parts of the same work of Marx and Engels may not refer to the same phase of Ancient Greek and Roman civilization. Therefore, identification of the specific phase should be carefully determined based on particular context rather than general assumptions. My textual analysis of the works of Marx and Engels indicate three major references by the terms "ancient" or "classical ancient."

First, the terms refer to the Ancient Greek and Roman people, nations, states, or world before the Middle Ages. Such references are more commonly used in

Marx's *Economic Manuscripts of 1857–1858* as seen here: "Among the ancients [Greeks and Romans], manufacture already appears as degeneration (an occupation fit only for freedmen, clients and foreigners), etc."[41] "The ancients" in this context refers to Ancient Greek and Roman people. Marx also said, In the ancient world, it is the city with its attached territory that forms the economic totality. Among the ancients (Romans as the classical example, the thing in its purest, most fully developed form) there is a contradiction between the form of State landed property and private landed property.[42] The term "ancient world" here refers to Ancient Greek and Roman world; "ancient nations" refer to Ancient Greek and Roman nations. In his 1853 *Forced Emigration.—Kossuth and Mazzini.—The Refugee Question.—Election Bribery in England.—Mr. Cobden*, Marx said,

> In the ancient States, in Greece and Rome, compulsory emigration, assuming the shape of the periodical establishment of colonies, formed a regular link in the structure of society. The whole system of those States was founded on certain limits to the numbers of the population, which could not be surpassed without endangering the condition of antique civilisation itself.[43]

"Ancient States" in this context refer to Ancient Greek and Roman states.

Marx's second reference of the terms is to Ancient Greek and Roman society in the time before slavery actually dominated production after dissolution of the primitive public ownership of land. In *Capital Volume I*, about the relations between (1) the capitalist cooperative and (2) smallholders and independent handicraft men, Marx said,

> Peasant agriculture on a small scale, and the carrying on of independent handicrafts, which together form the basis of the feudal mode of production, and after the dissolution of that system, continue side by side with the capitalist mode, also form the economic foundation of the classical communities at their best, after the primitive form of ownership of land in common had disappeared, and before slavery had seized on production in earnest.[44]

This has made it explicit that the peak of the "classical community" refers to the society after dissolution of the primitive common ownership of land and before slavery dominates production. It is a transitional form of society (rather than a slavery society) with the duality between public and private ownership and between the class and classless societies. The interpretation of the "classical community" as a slavery society represents a misunderstanding of Marx.

Here is a quote from Marx in his *Capital Volume III* about the emergence of capitalist land rent:

> This form of free self-managing peasant proprietorship of land parcels as the prevailing, normal form constitutes, on the one hand, the economic foundation of society during the best periods of classical antiquity, and on the other

> hand, it is found among modern nations as one of the forms arising from the dissolution of feudal land ownership.[45]

The best of "classical antiquity" here is the same society or period as the best of "classical community" mentioned previously in *Capital Volume I*, which is the time "before slavery actually dominated production after the dissolution of the primitive public ownership of land."

In his 1877 *Letter to Editor of the Otecestvenniye Zapisky*, Marx said,

> In several parts of *Capital* I allude to the fate which overtook the plebeians of ancient Rome. They were originally free peasants, each cultivating his own piece of land on his own account. In the course of Roman history they were expropriated. The same movement which divorced them from their means of production and subsistence involved the formation not only of big landed property but also of big money capital. And so one fine morning there were to be found on the one hand free men, stripped of everything except their labour power, and on the other, in order to exploit this labour, those who held all the acquired wealth in possession. What happened? The Roman proletarians became, not wage labourers but a mob of do-nothings; ...alongside of them there developed a mode of production which was not capitalist but dependent upon slavery.[46]

These quotations of Marx exactly refer to the transitioning from small-scale peasant economy at the heyday of "classical society" or "classical ancient society" to the slavery production mode.

The third reference of the terms is to the Ancient Greek and Roman slavery society. Engels said in chapter 8 of his *The Origin of the Family, Private Property and the State*,

> The slavery of classical times had outlived itself ... . Christianity is completely innocent of the gradual dying out of ancient slavery; it was itself actively involved in the system for centuries under the Roman Empire, and never interfered later with slave-trading by Christians: Not with the Germans in the north, or with the Venetians in the Mediterranean, or with the later trade in Negroes. Slavery no longer paid; it was for that reason it died out.[47]

He also said in chapter 9,

> With slavery, which attained its fullest development under civilization, came the first great cleavage of society into an exploiting and an exploited class. This cleavage persisted during the whole civilized period. Slavery is the first form of exploitation, the form peculiar to the ancient world; it is succeeded by serfdom in the middle ages, and wage labor in the more recent period. These are the three great forms of servitude, characteristic of the three great epochs of civilization; open, and in recent times disguised, slavery always accompanies them.[48]

Here the "ancient Greek and Roman time" and "classical ancient" refer to the slavery of Ancient Greek and Roman society. As argued by Engels, "slavery is the first form of exploitation peculiar to ancient Greek and Roman world."

In his 1887 article "The Labor Movement in America—Preface to the American Version of 'The Condition of the Working-Class in England'", Engels said, "In Asiatic and classical antiquity, the predominant form of class oppression was slavery, that is to say, not so much the expropriation of the masses from the land as the appropriation of their persons."[49] The term "Asiatic antiquity" does not refer to the Asiatic production mode and Asiatic community mentioned in the previous chapter "All forms of production prior to Capitalist production." Instead, it refers to the oriental slavery society derived from the Asian production mode and Asian community. "Classical antiquity" here refers to Ancient Greek and Roman slavery society.

As we know, Marx and Engels in their lifetime were only cognizant of the post-Homer Ancient Greek and Roman history, but unaware of Cretan civilization and Mycenaean civilization in 2000–1100 B.C. This is due to the fact that

> [o]ver a long period, people have been unaware of the existence of this ancient civilization until the archaeological excavation in the latter part of the 19th century, which completely rewrote the earliest chapters of the history of Greece thanks to the rediscovery of it.[50]

Cretan civilization and Mycenaean civilization had already been slavery societies. If counting from Cretan civilization and Mycenaean civilization, slavery society had existed for a long period in the history of Ancient Greek and Roman society. We can also say, in this sense, that the terms "ancient" or "classical ancient" are references to the slavery society in Ancient Greece and Rome in most cases.

2.2.4 The dissolution of pre-capitalistic social forms and the emergence of capitalism

As explained previously, the dissolution of all the primitive forms of ownership is the prerequisite for the emergence of capitalism. However, this dissolution alone does not furnish the conditions for the emergence of capitalism. The emergence of capitalism depends on the disintegration not only of all primitive ownerships but also of all derivative forms thereof. There are three major derivative forms of ownership generated after dissolution of the primitive ownerships. The first is that laborers become landowners, and work on their own land using their own production tools to own the products of their own work. This is the private ownership of small-scale peasant economy. The second derivative form is that laborers had their own production tools to produce what's for their own use or for sale. This is the private handicraft industry. Some wealthier private handicraftsmen become masters who employ apprentices, who in turn may later become handicraftsmen or masters themselves. The third derivative form is that laborers become owners of means of livelihood. These laborers are actually slaves and serfs, reliant on their owners, for whom they work and from whom they get their means of livelihood, which they can then use and allocate. Slavery and serf societies are two dominant derivative forms after the disintegration of primitive forms of ownership. Private peasant ownership and independent handicraftsmen rely on and thus acquire features of slavery or serfdom.

The derivative forms of ownership after the disintegration of primitive forms of ownership mentioned above share the following features. (1) There was no separation between laborers and the objective conditions of labor. As clearly observable, peasants and handicraftsmen were integrated with the objective conditions of labor. However, why was it that slavery and serfdom were also integrated with the objective conditions of labor since slaves and serfs did not even possess their own means of production (namely, the objective conditions of labor)? Marx thus answered this question in his article *Economic Manuscripts of 1857–1858*,

> In the relation of slavery and serfdom there is no such separation; rather, one part of society is treated by another as the mere *inorganic and natural* condition of its own reproduction. The slave stands in no relation whatsoever to the objective conditions of his labor; rather, *labor* itself, both in the form of the slave and of the serf, is *placed* along with the other natural beings such as cattle as an *inorganic condition* of production, as an appendage of the soil.[51]

(2) Use value and consumption-oriented production held an advantageous position. In other words, the direct purpose of production was use value instead of exchange value. Therefore, it was still a natural rather than commodity economy. (3) Personal attachment still existed. Slaves were attached to slave owners and serfs to serf owners. Apprentices and journeymen were not free so as to sell their hard work and labor for exchange with money. The derivative forms, due to their features as explained above, still lack the historical conditions for the emergence of capitalism, which needs to be predicated on the dissolution of the three derivative forms of ownership.

In the chapter "Bastiat and Carey" of *Economic Manuscripts of 1857–1858*, Marx criticized the four forms of wage labor,

> In real history, wage labour arises from the disintegration of slavery and serfdom—or from the decay of communal property as among the Oriental and Slav peoples—and, in its adequate, epoch-making form affecting the entire social existence of labour, from the decline of the guild economy, of the feudal estates system, of labour services and income in kind, of industry carried on as a rural sideline, of small-scale feudal agriculture, etc. In all these really historical transitions, wage labour appears as the dissolution, as the destruction of relations in which labour was fixed in all respects, in respect of income, content, locality, scope, etc. *Hence as negation of the fixity of labour and its remuneration.* The direct transition from the fetish of the African to Voltaire's être suprême or from the hunting gear of a North American savage

> to the capital of the Bank of England, is not as absurdly anti-historical as is Bastiat's transition from the fisherman to the wage labourer.[52]

Despite its long history and variety, the birth of wage labor did not equal the birth of the capitalistic mode of production. Engels explained in *Anti-Dühring*,

> [W]age-labour, which contains the whole capitalistic mode of production in embryo, is very ancient; in a sporadic, scattered form it existed for centuries alongside slave-labour. But the embryo could duly develop into the capitalistic mode of production only when the necessary historical preconditions had been furnished.[53]

Among the four forms of wage labor Engels mentioned, the first is from the disintegration of the slavery and serf system, the second from the collapse of oriental public ownership, the third from the decay of all forms of ownership, communities, economic systems, and hierarchy in Western feudal society, and the fourth is from Western capitalism's invasion and colonization of the primitive ownership in Africa and America. Among these four forms, the third typifies wage labor. Only wage labor generated from this form can duly develop into the capitalistic mode of production.

When discussing "the so-called primitive accumulation" in chapter 24 of *Capital Volume I*, Marx used England as a model to study in detail the historical process of the disintegration of the small peasant economy and the capitalist mode of production in the late feudal society. Marx said,

> In England, serfdom had practically disappeared in the last part of the 14th century. The immense majority of the population consisted then, and to a still larger extent, in the 15th century, of free peasant proprietors … . Although, therefore, the English land, after the Norman Conquest, was distributed in gigantic baronies, one of which often included some 900 of the old Anglo-Saxon lordships, it was bestrewn with small peasant properties.

The prelude of the revolution that laid the foundation for the capitalist mode of production kicked off in the last 30 years of the 15th century and the first few decades of the 16th century. At that time, the feudal lords, who fought against the royal family and the parliament, forcibly evicted the peasants from the land for seizing their common land, resulting in a large mass of proletariat.

> Even in the last decade of the 17th century, the yeomanry, the class of independent peasants, were more numerous than the class of farmers … . Even the serf was … also a co-possessor of the common land … . About 1750, the yeomanry had disappeared, and so had, in the last decade of the 18th century, the last trace of the common land of the agricultural labourer.[54]

This historical process fully shows that the deprivation of the production materials of the individual agriculturalist or individual yeoman separates them from the objective conditions of labor, which is the basic premise of the capitalist mode of production.

In the chapter concerning "various forms before the capitalist production," Marx attributed the causes, forms and processes of the capitalistic production to the following: (1) Only when both material productive forces and spiritual productive forces develop to a certain level can the capitalist mode of production be possible. This is because the emergence of the capitalist mode of production requires the disintegration of various pre-capitalist forms of ownership and communities, while the development of productive forces serves as the root cause of the disintegration of these forms of ownership and the communities. (2) Objective conditions of labor should be separated from laborers; thus, laborers can be free from all kinds of personal attachments and become proletarians with nothing but their own labor. Then they can freely sell their own labor, which is one of the important prerequisites for capitalism. Without laborers who can freely sell their own labor, the capitalist mode of production cannot emerge. (3) The purpose of capitalist production is not use value, but exchange value. Exchange value exists in the form of money. Only by accumulating enough money can a capitalist mode of production be produced. Because money can buy both the objective conditions of labor and the subjective conditions of labor, namely, the labor of free laborers. Marx claimed:

> It is inherent in the concept of capital—in its origin—that it begins with money, and therefore with wealth in the form of money. It is likewise inherent in it that it appears as emerging from circulation, as the product of circulation. Capital formation does not therefore arise from landed property … , nor from the guild … , but from merchants' and usurers' wealth. But this wealth only encounters the conditions which permit the purchase of free labour, once free labour has been detached from its objective conditions of existence as a result of an historical process. Only then does it also become possible to buy these conditions themselves.[55]

Here, Marx fully affirmed the important role of merchants, usurers, and the commodity economy in generating the capitalist mode of production. (4) The primitive accumulation of capital is an important link in the formation of the capitalist mode of production, which, Marx argues, may not be exactly what people think. It seems that capital accumulates living materials, labor tools, and raw materials. In a word, it accumulates objective conditions of labor which have been separated from the land and already included the human labor.

> Capital does not create the objective conditions of labour. Its original formation occurs simply because the historical process of the dissolution of the old mode of production enables value, existing in the form of monetary wealth, to buy the objective conditions of labour on the one hand, and to exchange the living labour of the now free workers for money on the other.[56]

Marx used Britain as an example to illustrate this point.

> For instance, when the great English landowners dismissed their retainers, who had consumed with them the surplus produce of their land; when their tenant farmers drove out the small cottagers, etc., then a mass of living labour power was thrown on to the labour market, a mass which was free in a double sense: Free from the old client or bondage relationships and any obligatory services, and free also from all goods and chattels, from every objective and material form of being, free from all property. It was reduced either to the sale of its labour capacity or to beggary, vagabondage or robbery as its only source of income.[57]

(5) The emergence of the capitalist mode of production was not just an economic process, in which violence also played an important role. In the chapter concerning "the so-called primitive accumulation" in *Capital Volume I*, Marx made this point explicit. He said:

> All methods of the primitive accumulation of capital employ the power of the State, the concentrated and organised force of society, to hasten, hot-house fashion, the process of transformation of the feudal mode of production into the capitalist mode, and to shorten the transition. Force is the midwife of every old society pregnant with a new one. It is itself an economic power.[58]

In short, Marx, in his second period, especially in "various forms before the capitalist production," also believed that the human society will in turn experience five social forms: Asiatic society, ancient society, feudal society, capitalist society, and communist society.

Let's compare Marx's thoughts of the second period with those of the first, to encapsulate the concept of the "Asiatic mode of production." In the early 1850s, Marx supported the special theory of the "Asiatic mode of production," which regarded the "Asiatic mode of production" as an independent, regional, and special social form. In the second period, although he didn't abandon the special theory of the "Asiatic mode of production," he no longer regarded the "Asiatic mode of production" as a special social form that cannot be placed at any stage of human history, but considered it as the first social form in human history. This social form is not the primitive society as we say nowadays, but with the dual features of both public- and private-owned societies, of both classless and class societies. It is a transitional social form between the primitive and the slave societies. The most primitive human society is the one we reference nowadays. Due to lack of historical materials, Marx and Engels didn't discover the "Asiatic mode of production" early on in their work. Engels' note in the English version of *The Communist Manifesto* in 1888 clearly explained this point. He said:

> In 1847, the pre-history of society, the social organisation existing previous to recorded history, all but unknown. Since then, August von Haxthausen

> (1792–1866) discovered common ownership of land in Russia, Georg Ludwig von Maurer proved it to be the social foundation from which all Teutonic races started in history, and, by and by, village communities were found to be, or to have been, the primitive form of society everywhere from India to Ireland. The inner organisation of this primitive communistic society was laid bare, in its typical form, by Lewis Henry Morgan's (1818–1861) crowning discovery of the true nature of the gens and its relation to the tribe. With the dissolution of the primeval communities, society begins to be differentiated into separate and finally antagonistic classes.[59]

That is to say, the most primitive stage of human society was revealed by Morgan's 1877 book *Ancient Society*. Therefore, it is unfounded to think that the "Asiatic mode of production" that Marx put forward in mid and late 1850s refers to the primitive society.

2.3 Period represented by *Capital*

This period lasted from the 1860s till 1877 when Marx and Engels discovered Morgan's book *Ancient Society*. A summary of key ideas of this period follows:

1. In *Capital* and other works, the "Asiatic mode of production" continues to be used as the first stage in human development, which is basically the same as the view in the second period.

Marx said in *Capital Volume I*:

> In the ancient Asiatic and other ancient modes of production, we find that the conversion of products into commodities, and therefore the conversion of men into producers of commodities, holds a subordinate place, which, however, increases in importance as the primitive communities approach nearer and nearer to their dissolution … . Those ancient social organisms of production are, as compared with bourgeois society, extremely simple and transparent. But they are founded either on the immature development of man individually, who has not yet severed the umbilical cord that unites him with his fellowmen in a primitive tribal community, or upon direct relations of subjection.[60]

Here, the "Asiatic mode of production" is still placed before the "ancient mode of production," and it points out "the immature development of man individually" and that man "has not yet severed the umbilical cord that unites him with his fellowmen" in the "Asiatic mode of production"; however, the "ancient mode of production" is "upon direct relations of subjection," namely slavery. It can be seen that Marx still believed that the "Asiatic mode of production" was a social form before the slave society.

Marx said in a note in *Capital Volume I*:

> Peasant agriculture on a small scale, and the carrying on of independent handicrafts, which together form the basis of the feudal mode of production, and after the dissolution of that system, continue side by side with the capitalist mode, also form the economic foundation of the classical communities at their best, after the primitive form of ownership of land in common had disappeared, and before slavery had seized on production in earnest.[61]

Here, "primitive form of ownership of land in common" stands for the "Asiatic mode of production." In this way, the "Asiatic mode of production," slavery, feudalism, and capitalism give exactly the four social forms in successive replacement before the communist society, in which the "Asiatic mode of production" stands as the first stage of the historical development. In addition, the best of "classical communities," as elaborated before, stands for the transitional period between the primitive common ownership of land and the slave society. It lies after the "Asiatic mode of production" and before the slavery society, but does to signify the slave society of Ancient Greece and Rome.

In *Capital Volume III*, Marx divided human history into four stages according to the level of commodity production, and regarded the "primitive community," including the "Asiatic mode of production," as the first stage of human history. When discussing commodity exchange and currency circulation, he said:

> No matter what the basis on which products are produced, which are thrown into circulation as commodities—whether the basis of the primitive community, of slave production, of small peasant and petty bourgeois, or the capitalist basis, the character of products as commodities is not altered, and as commodities they must pass through the process of exchange and its attendant changes of form.[62]

Here, "the primitive community" stands for primitive forms of ownership, including the "Asiatic mode of production"; the production based on "small peasant and petty bourgeois" means production modes in the feudal society. On this basis, the society based on the "Asiatic mode of production," slavery society, feudal society, and capitalist society again give exactly the four social forms in successive replacement before the communist society. With the addition of the communist society, we have a sequence of five social forms. Among these, the society based on the "Asiatic mode of production" acts as the first social form.

Engels wrote in *Anti-Dühring* (1876–1878) that, slavery society, serfdom / bondage, and wage labor serve as the three successive social forms in a class society. These, plus the social form before the slave society and the future communist society, again give us the sequence of five social forms.

As seen from the above paragraphs, Marx and Engels still adhered in their period to the theory of the successive replacement of five social forms, and regarded the "Asiatic mode of production" as the first social form of human history that existed before the slave society. It is groundless to believe that Marx and Engels in the period of *Capital* would regard the "Asiatic mode of production" as a social form that is contemporary with the slavery mode of production in Ancient Greece and Rome.

2. This period is different from the second period. Marx and Engels discovered the commonality in the historical development between Europe and Asia or the West and the East, and emphasized the universality of the "Asiatic mode of production," the first stage of human history. As a term for common ownership of land, the "Asiatic mode of production" exists in Ancient Europe as well as in Asia. Marx formed this opinion after reading the works of Georg Maurer.

Georg Maurer was once a parliamentary councilor of Bavaria, one of the regents of Greece, and a famous historian. In the 1850s and 1860s, he made a detailed survey of the Mark communes in Europe. Abundant historical data proved that there was common ownership of land in ancient Europe. Relics of this ownership still exist in countries of northwest Europe in different ways. Based on his research and study of the Mark, Maurer wrote a series of important historical works, including *Einleitung zur Geschichte der Mark-, Hof-, Dorf-, und Stadtverfassung und der offentlichen Gewalt* (Munich, 1854), *Geschichte der Markenverfassung in Deutschland* (Erlangen, 1856), and *Geschichte der Dorfverfassung in Deutschland* (Erlangen, 1865–1866). These works are all classics about the Mark commune. During his research at the British Museum, Marx saw these works and gave them high evaluation. He said in a letter to Engels on March 25, 1868, "His books are exceptionally important. Not only primitive times but the whole later development of the free imperial cities, the immunity of landowners, public authority and the struggle between free peasantry and serfdom is given an entirely new form." The discovery of Mark communes really excited Marx. A largely unnoticed issue had now become significant. In a highly delighted mood, Marx talked about the Mark communes, "Right in **my own** neighbourhood, on the **Hunsrücken**, the old Germanic system survived up till the **last** few years. I now remember my father talking to me about it from a **lawyer's** point of view."[63]

So, what is the relationship between the village system of Mark and the village system in India? In his letter to Engels of March 14, 1868, Marx said:

> It is interesting just now that the **Russian** manner of re-distributing land at certain intervals (in Germany originally annually) should have persisted in some parts of Germany up to the 18th century and even the 19th. The view I put forward that the Asiatic or Indian property forms everywhere mark the beginning in Europe receives new proof here (although Maurer know nothing of it). But for the Russians there disappears the last race OF ORIGINALITY, even in THIS Line. What remains to them is that they still maintain forms long abandoned by their neighbours.[64]

Here, Marx regarded the system of Mark as "the Asiatic or Indian property forms everywhere … in Europe," clearly indicating that Marx believed the village system of Mark and the village system of India to be essentially the same. The "Asiatic mode of production" has become synonymous with the public ownership of primitive land.

On the basis of considering the village system of Mark as essentially the same as the village system, Marx expanded the scope of communal ownership of rural land. By early 1870s, Marx further discovered that the existence of communal ownership of rural land is a universal phenomenon that has existed in every nation's history, and its appearance is of objective necessity—a logical and natural process of the historical development at that time.

Engels shared the same view with Marx. In his *On Social Relations in Russia* written in 1874–1875, Engels noted:

> In reality, communal ownership of the land is an institution found among all Indo-Germanic peoples at a low level of development, from India to Ireland, and even among the Malays, who are developing under Indian influence, for instance, on Java. As late as 1608, in the newly conquered North of Ireland, the legally established communal ownership of the land served the English as a pretext for declaring the land to be ownerless and, as such, escheated to the Crown. In India, a whole series of forms of communal ownership has been in existence down to the present time. In Germany it was general; the communal lands still to be found here and there are a relic of it; and often still distinct traces of it, temporary divisions of the communal lands, etc., are also to be found, especially in the mountains. More exact references and details with regard to old German communal ownership may be consulted in the various writings of Maurer, which are classic on this question. In Western Europe, including Poland and Little Russia, at a certain stage in social development, this communal ownership became a fetter, a brake on agricultural production, and was increasingly eliminated. In Great Russia (that is, Russia proper), on the other hand, it persists until today, thereby proving, in the first place, that here agricultural production and the social conditions in the countryside corresponding to it are still very undeveloped, as is actually the case.[65]

This shows that the Asiatic communal ownership of the land exists not only in Asian or Eastern countries, but also abundantly in the early stages of world history. In many places, it still preserves its remains. Thus, it is easy to find the commonality in the historical development of Europe, Asia, the West, and the East.

3. Marx and Engels discussed the differences between Eastern and Western societies in many works during this period. These discussions seem to be no different from and even a repetition of those in the 1850s. Yet, in reality, that's not the case. There are two obvious differences here:

First, in the early 1850s, the "Asiatic mode of production" was treated as an independent, regional, and special social formation. While, in the 1860s and 1870s, it was regarded as the first phase in human development.

Second, in the mid to late 1950s, in his chapter "Pre-capitalist Forms of Production" in *Economic Manuscripts of 1857–1858*, Marx discussed the characteristics of the "Asiatic mode of production" by comparing it with the classical ancient mode of production and the Germanic mode of production. But in the 1860s and 1870s, the characteristics of the "Asiatic mode of production" were discussed via comparison with the capitalist mode of production. And the characteristics of the "Asiatic mode of production" and the "Asian society" are considered relics of the ancient primitive communal ownership of land, relics visible not only in Asia but also in many parts of Europe. The difference is that Asia has the most and the most obvious relics. This can be seen clearly in the above quotation from *On Social Relations in Russia* by Engels and in Marx's letter to Engels in March 14, 1868. These characteristics fully demonstrate that in the 1860s and 1870s, Marx and Engels did not regard the "Asiatic mode of production" as an independent, regional, and special social formation that could not be placed in any stage of historical development. Further, it is not treated as a social formation that parallels the slave society and the feudal society, but as the first social formation in human history.

4. During this period, the "Asiatic mode of production" still does not refer to "the primitive human history," because science at that time had not yet furnished documentation about the primitive society.

In the second edition of the *Preface* to *Anti-Dühring* written on September 23, 1885, Engels once noted the exact revision he needed to make for the book. That is, Engels did not discuss the history of the primitive society until he wrote *Anti-Dühring* (1876–1878). He pointed out:

> First, to the history of primitive society, the key to which was provided by Morgan only in 1877. But as I have since then had the opportunity, in my work: *Der Ursprung der Familie, des Privateigenthums und des Stoats* (Zurich, 1884) to work up the material which in the meantime had become available to me, a reference to this later work meets the case.[66]

In short, in the 1860s and 1870s, Marx and Engels' views on the role of the "Asiatic mode of production" in human history were basically the same as those in the second period. "Asiatic mode of production" does not refer to the primitive society as it does now, but refers to the final stage of the primitive society. And this stage has the dual characteristics of a public and a private ownership society, and of a classless society and a class society. Marx and Engels regard the "Asiatic mode of production," the final stage of the primitive society, as an independent social formation in human history, indicating that their classification of social formations was not yet mature and in need of further development with updated historical documentation. In the following period, Marx and Engels discussed the history of primitive society, and used the scientific concept of the primitive society to replace the "Asiatic mode of production," "Asian society," and "Oriental society," thus finally completing their classification of the five social formations.

2.4 After Morgan's publication of *Ancient Society*

This period refers to the time when Marx and Engels witnessed Morgan's 1877 publication of *Ancient Society* until their death. Concerning their ideas in this period, two issues are especially noteworthy:

1. They affirmed the great achievements of Morgan's *Ancient Society*. Based on historical materials provided by Morgan and other sources, they illuminated the history of the primitive society. They scientifically ascertained the nature of the "Asiatic mode of production" and its role in human history. Thus, they consummated their classification of the five social forms.

In a letter to Karl Kautsky on April 26, 1884, Engels said:

> Morgan makes it possible for us to look at things from entirely new points of view by supplying us in his prehistory with a factual foundation that was missing hitherto. Whatever doubts you may still have about details in the history of primitive times and "savages", the gens settles the case in the main and explains the history of ancient society.[67]

In his 1884 *Preface* to edition 4 of *The Origin of the Family, Private Property and the State*, concerning Morgan's contribution to the study of primitive human history, Engels noted:

> Through the gens of the American Indians, he was enabled to make his second great advance in his field of research. In this gens, organized according to mother-right, he discovered the primitive form out of which had developed the later gens organized according to father-right, the gens as we find it among the ancient civilized peoples. The Greek and Roman gens, the old riddle of all historians, now found its explanation in the Indian gens, and a new foundation was thus laid for the whole of primitive history.

The above statements show that before the publication of Morgan's *Ancient Society*, Marx and Engels were only cognizant of the patriarchal gens of Ancient Greece and Rome and the agricultural commune derived from the gens (i.e., the classical ancient commune) and were of course also cognizant of the Asiatic commune and the Germanic commune that were contemporary with the classical ancient commune. In addition, they realized that the classical ancient commune was not the most primitive form of society. However, due to insufficient historical materials, the questions remain unresolved on how the Ancient Greek and Roman gens, the classical ancient commune, the Asiatic commune, and the Germanic commune emerged in history as well as what the social situation was like before their appearance. Marx and Engels only regarded these communes as the first stage of human history. Morgan's *Ancient Society*, by virtue of the materials based on the North American Indians, shows that the patriarchal gens of Ancient Greece and Rome evolved from the matriarchal gens, and that the Asiatic commune, the classical ancient commune, and the Germanic commune were formed from the disintegration of their respective patriarchal gens, and that these communes were not the most primitive forms of human society. *Ancient Society* scientifically ascertains their positions in human history, and completes the theory of the five social formations. Engels thus highly evaluated Morgan's research. Engels said:

> This rediscovery of the primitive matriarchal gens as the earlier stage of the patriarchal gens of civilized peoples has the same importance for anthropology as Darwin's theory of evolution has for biology and Marx's theory of surplus value for political economy. It enabled Morgan to outline for the first time a history of the family in which for the present, so far as the material now available permits, at least the classic stages of development in their main outlines are now determined. That this opens a new epoch in the treatment of primitive history must be clear to everyone. The matriarchal gens has become the pivot on which the whole science turns; since its discovery we know where to look and what to look for in our research, and how to arrange the results. And, consequently, since Morgan's book, progress in this field has been made at a far more rapid speed.[68]

On the role of the Asiatic, Classical Ancient, and Germanic communes in human history, Marx offered his explanation in the first draft of *Letter to Vera Zasulich*: "As the strata in geological structure, the configuration of history is composed of the prototypical form, the derivative form, and the sub-derivative form." These three forms of communes are not prototypical but derivative, giving the last stage of the primitive society. Marx continued:

> The rural commune therefore emerged in Germania from a more archaic type; it was the product of spontaneous development rather than being imported ready-made from Asia. It may also be found in Asia—in the East Indies—always as the final term or last period of the archaic formation.[69]

This clearly indicates that the Asiatic commune and the "Asiatic mode of production," like its contemporaries, including the classical ancient commune and the classical ancient mode of production, and the Germanic commune and Germanic mode of production, are the final stage of the primitive society. Before this, it was apparently inappropriate and unscientific for Marx to put one stage of the primitive society (namely the Asiatic commune and the "Asiatic mode of production" which is the last stage of the primitive society) as the first stage of human history. Therefore, the entire term of "primitive society" should replace those of "the Asiatic commune" and the "Asiatic mode of production."

Then, what are the features of the Asiatic, classical ancient, and Germanic communes (or rural communes or agricultural communes in Marxian terms) that distinguish them from the more archaic types of communes? Marx offered the following three features:

First, the earlier primitive communes all rested on the natural kinship of their members. After breaking this narrow but strong tie, the agricultural commune was able to expand themselves through greater contact with other communes.

Second, within the agricultural commune, the house and its appended land were already the farmer's private property, whereas the communal house was one of the material bases of previous communes, long before agriculture was even introduced.

Finally, although arable land remained communal property, it was periodically divided among the members of the agricultural commune, so that each farmer tilled the land allocated to them and individually appropriated their fruits. In the more archaic communities, by contrast, production was a common activity, and only the final produce was distributed among individual members. Of course, this more primitive type of collective or co-operative production stemmed from the weakness of the isolated individual, not from the collectivization of the means of production.

These three features indicated by Marx, although not reflective of the particularities of and differences among the Asiatic commune, the classical ancient commune, and the Germanic commune, offer a nice synopsis of their common features.

Marx believes that the agricultural commune had a dualism of double functions. First, it helped stabilize the communal property. Marx said:

> "The dualism" inherent in the "agricultural commune" may give it a sturdy life: for communal property and all the resulting social relations provide it with a solid foundation, while the privately owned houses, fragmented tillage of the arable land and private appropriation of its fruits all permit a development of individuality incompatible with conditions in the more primitive communities.

Second, it may become a source for the agricultural commune's dissolution. Marx said:

> Apart from the influence of a hostile environment, the mere accumulation over time of movable property, beginning with wealth in livestock and even extending to wealth in serfs, combines with the ever more prominent role played by movables in agriculture itself and with a host of other circumstances, inseparable from such accumulation, which would take me too far from the central theme. All these factors, then, serve to dissolve economic and social equality, generating within the commune itself a conflict of interests

> which leads, first, to the conversion of arable land into private property, and ultimately to the private appropriation of forests, pastures, waste ground, etc., already no more than communal appendages of private property.[70]

Marx's analysis here on the reasons and the process of the disintegration of the agricultural commune is much deeper and more specific than that of his in the mid to late 1950s.

Based on the dualism and its effect of the agricultural commune, Marx concluded:

> The "agricultural commune" everywhere presents itself as the most recent type of the archaic formation of societies; and the period of the agricultural commune appears in the historical course of Western Europe, both ancient and modern, as a period of transition from communal to private property, from the primary to the secondary formation.[71]

Therefore, Marx clearly believed that the rural communes, including the Asiatic commune, are the final stage of the primitive society and a transition from primary to secondary formations, from communal property to private property society, and from the classless society to class society.

In our investigation of Marxian thoughts of the second and third periods, we pointed out that the "Asiatic mode of production" that Marx put forward as the first stage of human history, does not refer to the entire primitive society, but to the final stage of it, a stage of transition from communal property society to private property society and from the classless society to class society. That was our analysis based on Marx's earlier argument before his formulation of a clearer conclusion. It was only in the fourth period that Marx for the first time made this direct and explicit conclusion. This is a major advancement and finalization of Marx's theory of five social formations.

2. After the disintegration of the primitive communes, their traces and communal land ownership remained everywhere, not only in Asia but also in Europe till the 18th and 19th centuries in certain countries. Just as we cannot claim that Europe did not go through the slave society or the feudal society because of the traces of the primitive communes and their communal land ownership in the continent, nor can we claim the same with Asia for the same reason. In 1882, Engels said in *The Mark*: "The old common property of all free men" only has a few traces

    > survived until our own time, but all through the Middle Ages they served as the basis and as the type of all public institutions and permeated the whole of public life, not only in Germany, but also in the north of France, England, and Scandinavia. And yet they have been so completely forgotten, that recently G. L. Maurer has had to re-discover their real significance … . The same primitive arrangement obtained until the beginning of this

> century in the so-called assignments by lot (Loosgüter) of the Rhein palatinate in Bavaria, whose arable land has since been turned into the private property of individuals. The Gehöferschaften also find it more and more to their interest to let the periodical redivision become obsolete and to turn the changing ownership into settled private property. Thus most of them, if not all, have died out in the last forty years and given place to villages with peasant proprietors using the forests and pasture land in common.[72]

In *The Frankish Period*, written in 1881–1882, Engels said:

> The Mark system remained the basis of almost the entire life of the German nation till the end of the Middle Ages. Eventually, after an existence of one and a half millennia, it gradually disintegrated for purely economic reasons. It succumbed to economic advances with which it was unable to keep pace.

But, "remnants of the Mark system continue to exist even today."[73]

Engels' above passages show that the German Mark system remained the basis of almost the entire life of the German nation until the end of the Middle Ages. The remnants of this system existed in northwestern Europe until the 19th century. We must not deny that there was a slave society and feudal society in Western Europe. In fact, no one has ever denied it. In the following we will examine the remnants of the "Asiatic mode of production" and compare them with the remnants of the Mark system in northwestern Europe to draw convincing conclusions.

In a letter to Karl Kautsky on February 16, 1884, Engels said that in Java and India, like in Russia, "primitive communism … supplies the best and also the broadest basis for exploitation and despotism, and survives in the midst of modern society as an anachronism … no less glaring than the Mark communities of the original cantons."[74] It is very clear here that the Asiatic communes have traces in Asia, just as the Mark communities have traces in northwestern Europe. Since people have never denied the fact that Europe had a slavery society and feudal society in spite of the existence of the Mark communities in northwestern Europe, why do people deny the existence of the slave society and the feudal society in Asia due to traces of the Asiatic communes in Asia? This obviously runs counter to logic and to historical facts.

In *The Origin of the Family, Private Property and the State*, Engels summarized the stages of historical development after the disintegration of the primitive society:

> With slavery, which attained its fullest development under civilization, came the first great cleavage of society into an exploiting and an exploited class. This cleavage persisted during the whole civilized period. Slavery is the first form of exploitation, the form peculiar to the ancient world; it is succeeded by serfdom in the middle ages, and wage-labor in the more recent period. These are the three great forms of servitude, characteristic of the three great epochs of civilization; open, and in recent times disguised, slavery always accompanies them.[75]

And Engels made it clear that slavery, serfdom, and wage labor are the three major forms of servitude characteristic of the three great epochs of civilization. These three forms of servitude existed not only in Europe, but also in Asia. The claim that there was no slavery in Asia contradicts Engels' argument. Engels also tells us that the three forms of servitude in different epochs of civilization have appeared one after another in history. The idea that slave society and feudal society are social forms spatially coexistent is at odds with Engels' argument.

Through the examination and analysis of the above two issues, let's briefly sum up the views of Marx and Engels in the fourth period:

First, the primitive society went through a series of stages before its final period. The Asiatic commune, the classical ancient commune, the Germanic commune, and their respective ownership systems were the final stages of the primitive society and the transitions form the primitive formation to a secondary formation, from a public ownership society to a private ownership society, and from a classless society to a class society. Therefore, the first stage of the human history should be the entire primitive society, not just the Asian society or the "Asiatic mode of production" which is merely the final stage of the primitive society. According to this view, the social evolutionary sequence in *Preface to A Contribution to the Critique of Political Economy* in 1859 should be revised, where the "Asiatic mode of production" should be replaced by "the primitive society."

Second, although the "Asiatic mode of production" as well as the Asian commune and the Indian commune, etc., like the Germanic Mark commune, were common in the Middle Ages, existing even till the 18th and 19th centuries in some regions, they were only relics of the ancient commune, rather than social formations that were different and independent territories parallel to the European society.

Third, human history has gone through three forms of servitude—slavery, feudalism, and capitalism. Preceding this sequence is the primitive society; and succeeding it is the communist society (with socialism as its first stage). Thus, human history has experienced and will experience five successive social forms—primitive society, slave society, feudal society, capitalist society, and communist society. Marx and Engels' theory of five social formations is hereto finally complete. It should be stated once again that the theory of five social formations I have discussed here is in respect to the entire world history. That is, the five social forms will occur in an inferior-to-superior succession in world history. It does not mean that a specific country or nation would undergo all the five social formations within itself regardless of its specific circumstances. In the development of world history, it is common for some countries and nations to skip one or more of the five social formations.

Based on our methodologies proposed above, we have examined the concept of the "Asiatic mode of production" and the evolution of its role as seen in Marx and Engels' works from the perspective of four periods. In connection with this, we have explained the gradual improvement of Marx and Engels' theory of five social formations. The whole evolutionary process can be summarized as follows.

In the mid to late 1840s, based on their study of European history, Marx and Engels divided human history into five successive social formations: tribal ownership society, slave society, feudal society, capitalist society, and communist society. In terms of economic structures, the tribal ownership system mentioned here is equivalent to the rural communes which appeared when the clan communes were dismantled and slavery began to appear. In the early 1850s, Marx and Engels began to study Asian society. As their perspectives broadened from Europe to Asia, historical materials they had were not sufficient or accurate. In addition, they were theoretically influenced by special theories of oriental societies of Aristotle and Hegel, so they were limited to the uniqueness of Asian society and did not find out the law of social development common for both Europe and Asia. They did not put Asian society in human historical sequence, but rather regarded it as an independent, regional, and special social formation entirely different from the Western society.

In the second and third periods, Marx and Engels still held onto their thought of the Particularism of Asian Society, though they no longer regarded the "Asiatic mode of production" as an independent, regional, and special social formation. Instead, they viewed it as the first stage in human social development, and believed that human history consists of five social formations, which are in succession: The society based on the "Asiatic mode of production," slave society, feudal society, capitalist society, and communist society (with socialist society as its first stage).

In the fourth period, based on research findings about the primitive history provided by Morgan's *Ancient Society* and other historical materials, Marx and Engels definitely concluded that the society based on the "Asiatic mode of production" is the last stage of the primitive society. That is, human society would transit from the public ownership society to the private ownership society, from a classless society to a class society. As a result, they regarded the remnant "Asiatic mode of production" as the relic of the primitive society, and used "primitive society" in place of "the society based on the Asiatic mode of production" for their classification of the five social formations.

Our investigations up to now have clearly indicated that the classification of five social formations was proposed by Marx and Engels in the mid-1840s and finally completed in the late 1870s to 1880s. This theory runs through the representative works of Marx and Engels, including *The German Ideology*, *Manifesto of the Communist Party*, *Wage Labour and Capital, Economic Manuscripts of 1857–1858*, *Preface to A Contribution to the Critique of Political Economy*, *Capital*, *Anti-Dühring*, and *The Origin of the Family, Private Property and the State*. Lenin also discussed in many of his works that the five social formations develop in an inferior-to-superior succession. In 1938, Joseph Stalin simply re-raised and developed the thoughts of Marx, Engels, and Lenin in his work *Dialectical and Historical Materialism*. Some people distorted the theory of the five social formations founded by Marx and Engels by claiming that it was first proposed by Stalin, and on that ground denied the theory as Marxian. This view is completely untenable.

Notes

1 *An Anthology of Marx and Engels* (Vol. 1). (2009). Beijing, China: People's Publishing House, 521.
2 *An Anthology of Marx and Engels* (Vol. 1). (2009). Beijing, China: People's Publishing House, 521–523.
3 *An Anthology of Marx and Engels* (Vol. 1). (2009). Beijing, China: People's Publishing House, 521.
4 *An Anthology of Marx and Engels* (Vol. 1). (2009). Beijing, China: People's Publishing House, 724.
5 *An Anthology of Marx and Engels* (Vol. 1). (2009). Beijing, China: People's Publishing House, 31.
6 *An Anthology of Marx and Engels* (Vol. 1). (2009). Beijing, China: People's Publishing House, 32.
7 *An Anthology of Marx and Engels* (Vol. 2). (2009). Beijing, China: People's Publishing House, 612.
8 *An Anthology of Marx and Engels* (Vol. 10). (2009). Beijing, China: People's Publishing House, 112.
9 *An Anthology of Marx and Engels* (Vol. 10). (2009). Beijing, China: People's Publishing House, 113.
10 *An Anthology of Marx and Engels* (Vol. 2). (2009). Beijing, China: People's Publishing House, 679.
11 Bernier, F. (1916). *Travels in the Mogul Empire*. Oxford, England: Oxford University Press, 204, 211, 224.
12 De Montesquieu, B. (1961). *The Spirit of the Laws* (Zhang Yanshen, Trans.). Vol. 1. Beijing, China: The Commercial Press.
13 Smith, A. (1974). *An Inquiry into the Nature and Causes of the Wealth of Nations* (Yang Jingnian, Trans.). Vol. 2. Beijing, China: The Commercial Press.
14 Ji Xianlin (1979). *An Insight into Ramayana*. Beijing, China: Foreign Literature Publishing House, 7.
15 *An Anthology of Marx and Engels* (Vol. 9). (2009). Beijing, China: People's Publishing House, 357.
16 *An Anthology of Marx and Engels* (Vol. 9). (2009). Beijing, China: People's Publishing House, 145.
17 *Collected Works of Marx and Engels* (Vol. 45). (1985). Beijing, China: People's Publishing House, 242–243.
18 *An Anthology of Marx and Engels* (Vol. 2). (2009). Beijing, China: People's Publishing House, 681, 682.
19 *Collected Works of Marx and Engels* (Vol. 28). (1973). Beijing, China: People's Publishing House.
20 *An Anthology of Marx and Engels* (Vol. 2). (2009). Beijing, China: People's Publishing House, 679–680.
21 *Collected Works of Marx and Engels* (Vol. 30). (1995). Beijing, China: People's Publishing House, 471–472. Emphasis added.
22 *Collected Works of Marx and Engels* (Vol. 30). (1995). Beijing, China: People's Publishing House, 469–475.
23 *Collected Works of Marx and Engels* (Vol. 30). (1995). Beijing, China: People's Publishing House, 475.
24 *Collected Works of Marx and Engels* (Vol. 30). (1995). Beijing, China: People's Publishing House, 477–478.
25 *Collected Works of Marx and Engels* (Vol. 30). (1995). Beijing, China: People's Publishing House, 476.
26 *Collected Works of Marx and Engels* (Vol. 30). (1995). Beijing, China: People's Publishing House, 468. Emphasis added.

27 *Collected Works of Marx and Engels* (Vol. 30). (1995). Beijing, China: People's Publishing House, 374, 473.
28 *Collected Works of Marx and Engels* (Vol. 30). (1995). Beijing, China: People's Publishing House, 478.
29 *Collected Works of Marx and Engels* (Vol. 30). (1995). Beijing, China: People's Publishing House, 478.
30 *Collected Works of Marx and Engels* (Vol. 30). (1995). Beijing, China: People's Publishing House, 475.
31 *Collected Works of Marx and Engels* (Vol. 30). (1995). Beijing, China: People's Publishing House, 475.
32 *Collected Works of Marx and Engels* (Vol. 30). (1995). Beijing, China: People's Publishing House, 476.
33 *Collected Works of Marx and Engels* (Vol. 30). (1995). Beijing, China: People's Publishing House, 484.
34 *Collected Works of Marx and Engels* (Vol. 35). (1971). Beijing, China: People's Publishing House, 131.
35 *Collected Works of Marx and Engels* (Vol. 30). (1995). Beijing, China: People's Publishing House, 486–487.
36 *Collected Works of Marx and Engels* (Vol. 30). (1995). Beijing, China: People's Publishing House, 487.
37 *Collected Works of Marx and Engels* (Vol. 30). (1995). Beijing, China: People's Publishing House, 487.
38 *Collected Works of Marx and Engels* (Vol. 30). (1995). Beijing, China: People's Publishing House, 473–474.
39 Wu Yuqin & Qi Shirong (Eds.) (1994). *World History-Ancient History Series.* (Vol.1). Beijing, China: Higher Education Press, 90–91.
40 Zhu Longhua (1991). *World History—Ancient Part.* Beijing, China: Peking University Press, 430–431.
41 *Collected Works of Marx and Engels* (Vol. 30). (1995). Beijing, China: People's Publishing House, 487.
42 *Collected Works of Marx and Engels* (Vol. 30). (1995). Beijing, China: People's Publishing House, 475.
43 *Collected Works of Marx and Engels* (Vol. 8). (1961). Beijing, China: People's Publishing House, 618–619.
44 *An Anthology of Marx and Engels* (Vol. 5). (2009). Beijing, China: People's Publishing House, 388.
45 *An Anthology of Marx and Engels* (Vol. 7). (2009). Beijing, China: People's Publishing House, 911.
46 *An Anthology of Marx and Engels* (Vol. 3). (2009). Beijing, China: People's Publishing House, 66.
47 *An Anthology of Marx and Engels* (Vol. 4). (2009). Beijing, China: People's Publishing House, 169.
48 *An Anthology of Marx and Engels* (Vol. 4). (2009). Beijing, China: People's Publishing House, 195.
49 *Collected Works of Marx and Engels* (Vol. 4). (1995). Beijing, China: People's Publishing House, 391.
50 Zhu Longhua (1991). *World History—Ancient Part.* Beijing, China: Peking University Press, 318.
51 *Collected Works of Marx and Engels* (Vol. 30). (1995). Beijing, China: People's Publishing House, 481. Emphasis added.
52 *Collected Works of Marx and Engels* (Vol. 30). (1995). Beijing, China: People's Publishing House, 15. Emphasis added.

53 *An Anthology of Marx and Engels* (Vol. 9). (2009). Beijing, China: People's Publishing House, 287.
54 *An Anthology of Marx and Engels* (Vol. 5). (2009). Beijing, China: People's Publishing House, 823–824, 824–825, 825, 830.
55 *Collected Works of Marx and Engels* (Vol. 30). (1995). Beijing, China: People's Publishing House, 499.
56 *Collected Works of Marx and Engels* (Vol. 30). (1995). Beijing, China: People's Publishing House, 501.
57 *Collected Works of Marx and Engels* (Vol. 30). (1995). Beijing, China: People's Publishing House, 502.
58 *An Anthology of Marx and Engels* (Vol. 5). (2009). Beijing, China: People's Publishing House, 861.
59 *An Anthology of Marx and Engels* (Vol. 2). (2009). Beijing, China: People's Publishing House, 31.
60 *An Anthology of Marx and Engels* (Vol. 5). (2009). Beijing, China: People's Publishing House, 97.
61 *An Anthology of Marx and Engels* (Vol. 5). (2009). Beijing, China: People's Publishing House, 388.
62 *An Anthology of Marx and Engels* (Vol. 7). (2009). Beijing, China: People's Publishing House, 362–363.
63 *An Anthology of Marx and Engels* (Vol. 10). (2009). Beijing, China: People's Publishing House, 283–284. Emphasis added.
64 *An Anthology of Marx and Engels* (Vol. 10). (2009). Beijing, China: People's Publishing House, 281–282. Emphasis added.
65 *An Anthology of Marx and Engels* (Vol. 3). (2009). Beijing, China: People's Publishing House, 396–397.
66 *An Anthology of Marx and Engels* (Vol. 9). (2009). Beijing, China: People's Publishing House, 12–13.
67 *An Anthology of Marx and Engels* (Vol. 10). (2009). Beijing, China: People's Publishing House, 516.
68 *An Anthology of Marx and Engels* (Vol. 3). (2009). Beijing, China: People's Publishing House, 28.
69 *An Anthology of Marx and Engels* (Vol. 3). (2009). Beijing, China: People's Publishing House, 573, 581.
70 *An Anthology of Marx and Engels* (Vol. 3). (2009). Beijing, China: People's Publishing House, 574.
71 *An Anthology of Marx and Engels* (Vol. 3). (2009). Beijing, China: People's Publishing House, 574.
72 *Collected Works of Marx and Engels* (Vol. 19). (1963). Beijing, China: People's Publishing House, 355–356.
73 *Collected Works of Marx and Engels* (Vol. 19). (1963). Beijing, China: People's Publishing House, 539.
74 *Collected Works of Marx and Engels* (Vol. 36). (1974). Beijing, China: People's Publishing House, 112.
75 *An Anthology of Marx and Engels* (Vol. 4). (2009). Beijing, China: People's Publishing House, 195.

3 A comparison of Eastern and Western ancient societies

The historical development of different countries and nations has both generality and individuality. The generality illustrates the common nature, general laws, objective inevitability and other characteristics of the historical development, and cannot encompass the entirety, uniqueness, and differences of and between different countries' histories. Therefore, the principle of generality of historical development is not a panacea for explaining the historical development of each country or nation. In order to specify the history of each country or nation, it is necessary to study the diversity of their historical development. In this chapter, following the principle of generality of historical development, we will focus on the differences in the ancient history of the East and the West. The ancient society includes three social formations: primitive society, slave society, and feudal society. The primitive society is of a long and distant history and often is inadequately documented, which poses challenges to our work here. Consequently, the chapter will give greater focus on the different characteristics of slave society and feudal society between the East and the West.

3.1 Different characteristics of slavery and feudalism in the East and the West

3.1.1 Status of slave society in world history

Which countries in the East did or did not experience slave society? Has slave society ever existed in China? If so, what was its duration? If we deny that slave society once existed, what is the basis of that denial? Historians' answers diverge on these questions. As a scholar of philosophical researches, I am unable to solve such controversy. Based on "Ancient Times" in *World History* edited by Wu Yuqin and Qi Shirong, I will analyze whether slave society existed in ancient Egypt, Mesopotamia, and India. In Egypt, from 4000 B.C. to 3500 B.C.., private ownership and production relations began to emerge. From 3500 B.C. to 3100 B.C., private ownership was gradually established, and classes were gradually formed. In the period of the ancient kingdom, also known as the pyramid period (2686–2181 B.C.), the slave economy was greatly developed. By the time of New Kingdom (1570–1085 B.C.), Egypt had already developed into a strong slave country. Over a period of about 100 years, the kings of Egypt led their army in battles across the country, expanding Egypt into a slavery empire across West Asia and North Africa. Their war conquests brought an influx of wealth and labor into Egypt, greatly promoting its slave economy. Compared with the Old Kingdom period, the composition of government officials in the New Kingdom period underwent major changes. Bureaucrats were selected not only from the royal family and imperial household, but more often from the entire ruling class. This enlarged the class foundation of the autocratic monarchy during the New Kingdom period and changed the composition of Egyptian slave owners and grew them into a mature class. At this time, the autocratic monarchy system had been established due to the long and deep development of slavery and the emergence of an entire slave owner class. The New Kingdom was the regime no longer of the royal family, nor of nobles, but of the entire slave owner class. Thus, Egypt did experience the slave society.

In Mesopotamia, the Sumerians experienced the disintegration of the clan society and its transition into the civilized period from about 4300 B.C. The city-states of Sumer were formed with the city center surrounded by villages and towns. The early city-states were small. For example, the city of Ur had an area of only 90 square kilometers and a population of about 6,000. Each city had several temples, of which the Lord God's temple of city-state held the highest position. Temples played an important role in the economic life of Sumer's city-states and were also the economic center of the city-states. The temple economy had finer internal division of labor, including agriculture, animal husbandry, fishing, etc. Temples also controlled the handicraft industry and commerce of city-states. Temples relied on slave labor, where some slaves belonged to the temples, while others to the managers of the temple. The temple economy was controlled by the slave owners and nobles headed by city-state leaders. They held a large amount of land, while the lowest slaves lived on bare subsistence. What's more, the slaveholders headed by city-state leaders also occupied a large number of sacred temple fields, or they combined their individual lands with sacred fields, all cultivated by temple dependents and slaves. In the late period of the Early Dynasty, with the development of slavery, class struggle within the city-state sharpened. During the dynasty of Akkad (2371–2191 B.C.), slavery was further developed. Protracted foreign wars turned a large number of war prisoners into slaves. In the third dynasty of Ur (2113–2006 B.C.), slave trading was common. Ordinary shepherds, craftsmen, merchants, and soldiers all owned slaves. During the period of the Babylonian Kingdom, royal families owned a large number of slaves. So did wealthy freemen with citizenship rights. In addition to war prisoners as a source, slaves were also purchased from other places. Slave trade was common. In Assyria, the Hittite Kingdom that emerged in 2000 B.C. was a slavery power. The *Hittite Code* indicated the existence of slavery in Hittite. These slaves, many formerly as war prisoners, engaged in agriculture, handicrafts, housework, and grazing livestock. During the New Babylonian period (612–539 B.C.), slavery developed further. Not only had the number of slaves increased, but the forms of exploitation of the slaves diversified. The above review clearly describes Mesopotamia as a slave society.

India's Habalah culture dates from 2300 B.C. to 1750 B.C. Specifically, its central area dates from 2300 B.C. to 2000 B.C., and its peripheral areas date from about 2200 B.C. to 1700 B.C. Ancient India entered civilization during the Habalah culture. Agriculture, handicrafts, and commerce were developed to an extent. Rudimentary private ownership began to emerge. During the Vedic period (1500 B.C. to 600 B.C.) in India, with the advent of private ownership, the gap between rich and poor began to widen. Those poor that could not make a living had to borrow from the rich. If unable to repay the debt, they had to offer forced labor. The rich exploited not only the debtors but also the slaves. The source of slavery was not limited to prisoners of wars. Those who lost a wager or could not repay their debts would also become slaves. Slaves had to engage in agriculture, handicrafts, animal husbandry, and so on for their masters. During the era of the 16 great states (6 B.C. to 2 B.C.), with the development of the commodity economy, society underwent great differentiation. People of the four castes experienced polarization between the rich and the poor, so that their original caste status may have no longer reflected a person's actual class status. Among the four castes, Brahman was the highest. During this period, some people became slave owners, while others fell as slaves. The second caste was Kshatriya, headed by the king, among whom some experienced a drop in status. They were occupied in agriculture, handicrafts, business, and other lowly occupations. The third caste was Vaisya, who were originally the general civilians. But at this time, some Vaisya became rich (e.g., rich merchants and loan sharks), while others lost their small plots of land and had to engage in lower occupations. As for the lowest Sudra in the four castes, a few made a fortune and became donors to Buddhism, while others degenerated into "untouchables." In the era of the 16 great states, India's slavery developed significantly. The slaves were used in the king's court and in aristocratic families, for domestic work, and for agricultural production. The above brief review describes India as a slave society.

Whether slave society has existed in Chinese history is a more complicated issue. People hold diametrical views. Those with an affirmative answer, however, disagree on the durations of it. The controversy may closely relate to another question—when did China enter feudal society? There are seven main different views on this last question, giving seven different times for the start of China's feudal society: (1) The Western Zhou Dynasty (e.g., as argued by Fan Wenlan and Jian Bozan); (2) the Spring and Autumn Period (e.g., Li Yanong and Tang Lan); (3) the Warring States Period (e.g., Guo Moruo and Wu Dakun); (4) China's reunification in Qin Dynasty; (5) the Western Han Dynasty (e.g., Hou Wailu); (6) the Eastern Han Dynasty (e.g., Zhou Gucheng); and (7) the Wei-jin Period (e.g., Shang Yue and Wang Zhongluo). This controversy necessarily leads to the controversy over the end time of the slave society. In addition, Lei Haizong, Li Hongzhe, and others deny that China ever went through the slave society and believe that the beginning of Chinese civilization was feudal society.[1] Li Hongzhe believes that many peoples and nations in world history went straight from the primitive society to the feudal society, such as Slavs, Germanic people, Aztec, Georgia, Inca, Egypt, Mesopotamia, India. The same is true with China.

Therefore, he argues that the belief of the existence of slavery society in China is theoretically untenable and does not conform to historical facts. Li's belief has been generally endorsed for years and has become almost dogmatic.[2] I contend that despite the above controversies, slavery appeared in all disintegrations of the primitive society, which is an undeniable fact. The difference lies in whether slavery as a mode of production assumed a dominant position. For countries and regions where the slavery mode of production played a leading role, we can say that slave society existed there. However, for those where slavery did not play a leading role, it may be conceded that slavery was nonexistent there. Therefore, we will not discuss different characteristics of the *slave society* in the East and West but will explore different characteristics of Eastern and Western *slavery*. By doing so, we hope to evade certain major disputes.

The disintegration of primitive communities and the formation of slavery in all countries and nations are, ultimately, results of the development of productive forces and the contradiction between productive forces and production relations. Slavery in all countries and nations is compatible with a certain stage of productivity. However, different natural conditions and social conditions in the East and the West led to differences in slavery at different locations after dissolution of the primitive society. For example, in Western Europe, slavery was introduced with the invention and application of ironware; while in China, slavery came in the wake of the manufacture and use of bronze. To be specific, in Western Europe, social division under slavery was relatively high, and commodity production and exchange were relatively developed. In ancient Greece, there had been relatively developed overseas trade; while in China social division of labor was relatively low, commodity production and exchange were less developed. China's economy was largely of the natural self-sufficient type combining agriculture and handicraft industry.

In the production relations of any kind of slavery, slave owners possessed the means of production as well as the production workers—the slaves, used not unlike livestock, for the slave trade and even for slaughter. However, slave owners may have possessed the production means and labor in varied forms and conditions. Those in Western Europe mainly practiced a private land ownership. Those in the East, such as China and India, mainly practiced state ownership of land (aka the co-ownership by slave owners). The "grid-field system (the 'nine squares' system of land ownership in China's slave society with one large square divided into nine small ones, resembling the Chinese character 井)" in China's Western Zhou Dynasty was a typical example of such land ownership. In terms of the possession of slaves, private slaves were mainly used in Western Europe, while states' slaves were used more often in the East; unmarried slaves were often used in the West while in the East, in addition to unmarried slaves, slaves with families were used more often; most of the slaves in the West were chattel slaves (or slaves without family property). Bonded slaves were merely used during the late Roman Empire, while the same were used earlier and more often in the East. In addition, slaves accounted for different proportions of the populations in Eastern and Western slavery countries. In Western Europe, slaves accounted for a larger proportion of the total population; while in the East, they accounted for a smaller proportion.

Because of the basic characteristics of the slavery production relations—slave owners possessed both the means of production and the slaves—their exploitation and oppression of the slaves was uniformly cruel. However, slavery varied geographically in its characteristics, exploitations, and developments. For example, in Western Europe, slave owners mainly operated large manors or workshops, and coerced slaves into massive collective labor; while in the East, slave owners mainly divided lands into small plots distributed to slaves with families, who would engage in individual farming as a family unit. In addition, slaves were used for housework more often in the East. What is significant in New Babylon is that the

> independent operation by slaves is frequently adopted, that is, slave owners give slaves a part of property (including lands and funds) and allow them to manage the property independently. Slaves can independently rent land, go into business, engage in handicraft manufacturing and operate manual workshop, or even start money shops for moneylending, etc. Not only can private slaves operate independently, but also slaves of temples can do the same … . Among such slaves with the permission of independent operation, some of them may obtain a quite high level of wealth, and even have slaves. Slaves sometimes act as agents of their owners to engage in various economic activities while managing their own business. During their engagement in various activities for their masters, they receive wages from the slave owners as reward … . [However], among slaves capable of independent operation, only a few of them can become rich; and these wealthy slaves are still their masters' property, their masters can dispose of them optionally for trade, transfer, or acting as a dowry.[3]

Slave owners everywhere forced slaves into productive labor such as agriculture, handicrafts, and animal husbandry. However, slave labor assumed different positions in social production in different locations. In Western Europe, slave owners drove a large number of slaves into all types of productive labor. Slave labor dominated productive labor. While in some countries or during certain periods in the East, slave labor did not dominate the productive labor. For example, in the early Vedic era of India, slave labor "only occupied an auxiliary secondary position in productive labor of society, and main labor producers were free members of clan tribes."[4] For another example, during the New Babylonian Kingdom in Mesopotamia, although

> the number of slaves was quite large, they were not main producers. The main producers at that time were a large number of free people who lost their means of production. They rented land from royal houses, temples and individual slave owners, and often needed to rent livestock, seeds and farm tools. They were also the main exploitees at the time.[5]

In still another example, after the Persian Empire conquered Babylonia, literature shows that

> the unique way of exploiting slaves during the New Babylonian kingdom, that is, the way in which slaves operate independently, still existed during the Persian Empire. Egibi merchants and Mugla merchants have saved information on such kind of slave exploitation. In Babylonia, just as before the Persian conquest, the main exploitees, except for slaves enduring exploitation, were Erresu who were formally free and worked on the land of various slave owners under the supervision of supervisors.[6]

In view of the above differences of slavery in Western Europe (ancient Greece and Rome) and ancient Eastern countries, people naturally regard slavery in these two regions as two types of slavery, which undoubtedly is correct. However, it should also be noted that slavery in ancient Greece and Rome differed from each other; and slavery in ancient Eastern countries also had differences between, for instance, Chinese slavery and Indian slavery. Besides, in diverse regions of the same slavery country, there may be different types of slavery. For example, in ancient Greece, slavery in Athens was of the industrial and commercial city-state type and that in Sparta, the agricultural city-state type. If we compare slavery established earlier in ancient Greece and later collapsed Crete and Mycenae with the slavery of Greece and Rome which was established later, the difference becomes even more pronounced.

3.1.2 Different characteristics of feudal societies in the East and West

For all feudal countries, as their predominant production relations, feudal lords possessed production materials and partially production laborers—serfs or peasants. Serfs or peasants had certain personal attachments to feudal lords. However, in feudal societies of different countries and nations, due to diverse natural and social conditions and levels of productivity, land ownerships as the basis of feudal production relations were different. For instance, feudal land in Western Europe was held mainly by feudal lords while in the East, feudal state land ownership and feudal landlord land ownership coexisted. Further, the specific conditions of peasants as exploitees by the feudal lords were different. In Western Europe, serfs were the main targets of exploitation with strong dependence on their owners; in the East, private tenant peasants and state tenant peasants were exploited more, with a weaker dependence on their feudal lords. In addition, feudal lords' exploitation methods differed in the East and the West. In Western Europe, labor rent was dominant, while in the East it was produce rent. We will next analyze the feudal class relations and feudal exploitation methods under the state ownership of feudal land.

In reference to labor ground rent, Marx in chapter 47 "Genesis of Capitalist Ground-Rent" of *Capital Volume III* stated:

> Should the direct producers not be confronted by a private landowner, but rather, as in Asia, under direct subordination to a state which stands over them

> as their landlord and simultaneously as sovereign, then rent and taxes coincide, or rather, there exists no tax which differs from this form of ground rent. Under such circumstances, there need exist no stronger political or economic pressure than that common to all subjection to that state. The state is then the supreme lord. Sovereignty here consists in the ownership of land concentrated on a national scale. But, on the other hand, no private ownership of land exists, although there is both private and common possession and use of land.[7]

Some scholars in China dichotomize Marx's state land ownership and feudal land ownership, believing that it is neither the land ownership of slavery nor the feudal land ownership, but rather a special form of land ownership. They then describe the Asian society as a special, regional, and independent social formation and ignore the fact that Asian countries and nations have experienced the slave society and the feudal society, thus denying Marx's theory of successive replacement of the five social formations. This view is completely untenable. In fact, what Marx referred to is exactly the two forms of feudal land ownership, to wit, the private ownership of feudal land and the state ownership of feudal land. Compared with the private ownership of feudal land, the state ownership of feudal land certainly can be regarded as a special form of land ownership, which, however, is a special form still of a feudal nature rather than another form of land ownership fundamentally different from feudal land ownership. Marx's above quote has made this explicit. He continues:

> It is always the direct relationship of the owners of the conditions of production to the direct producers—a relation always naturally corresponding to a definite stage in the development of the methods of labour and thereby its social productivity—which reveals the innermost secret, the hidden basis of the entire social structure and with it the political form of the relation of sovereignty and dependence, in short, the corresponding specific form of the state. This does not prevent the same economic basis—the same from the standpoint of its main conditions—due to innumerable different empirical circumstances, natural environment, racial relations, external historical influences, etc. from showing infinite variations and gradations in appearance, which can be ascertained only by analysis of the empirically given circumstances.[8]

Here, Marx argues that private ownership and state ownership are two different forms of feudal land ownership which belong to "the standpoint of its main conditions" and "the same economic basis" of the feudal society. The two forms of ownership differ only in "variations and gradations," "in appearance." Because of economics "variations and gradations," the political superstructure built on the economy also has different characteristics. To regard the private ownership of feudal land and the state ownership of feudal land as two distinct economic bases or as two different categories of production relations is contrary to Marx's original intention.

In the following, we will elaborate the commonalities and differences between the private ownership and state ownership of feudal land as in reference to Marx's discussion.

First, these two types of land ownership are different from the slavery economy, under which slaves used other means of production to realize their labor and such labor was not independent. Under the private ownership of feudal land, the direct producer was independent, and

> the direct producer, according to our assumption, is to be found here in possession of his own means of production, the necessary material labour conditions required for the realisation of his labour and the production of his means of subsistence. He conducts his agricultural activities and the rural home industries connected with it independently.

Under the state ownership of feudal land, these direct laborers "may form among themselves a more or less natural production community," but their independence will not "be undermined."[9] This indicates that despite certain differences between the private ownership and state ownership of feudal land, the two are essentially the same, and fundamentally distinct from the slavery economy.

Second, both types of land ownership are subject to supra-economic compulsory labor, have certain relations of bondage, have a certain degree of personal freedom and attachment to the land as an appurtenant to the land, and must have an authentic class of dependent peasants. Their difference lies in the degree of personal attachment, which is stronger under the private ownership of feudal land than under the state ownership of feudal land. As Marx puts it, under the state ownership of feudal land, "there need exist no stronger political or economic pressure than that common to all subjection to that state."

Third, under these two categories of land ownership, laborers must pay rents or taxes to the exploiters or the states and dedicate their surplus labor gratis to the feudal lord class and the state. The difference is that under the private ownership of feudal land, the rent and tax were separate. The laborer pays the tax to the state and the land rent to the landowner. Under the state ownership of feudal land, as Marx said: "rent and taxes coincide, or rather, there exists no tax which differs from this form of ground-rent."

In short, the state ownership of feudal land, which embodies basic characteristics of the feudal economic system, is a concrete form of the feudal land ownership and should not be excluded from it. It cannot be argued that Asia did not experience the slave society and the feudal society because of the existence of the state ownership of feudal land in Asia.

3.2 Typical developments of Eastern and Western slavery and feudalism

Although we believe some countries in the East and West have experienced successively the slave society and the feudal society, we at the same time hold that not all countries have developed the typical slave and feudal societies. Due to different natural and social conditions of each country and external influences, the historical progress of each country cannot be uniform. A country may be typical in one social form but lags behind or remains weak in another. Different social forms in different countries may assume different significance. Ancient Greece and Rome, as we understand, were typical examples of the slavery society; while China was a typical feudal society.

3.2.1 Typical examples of the slavery society

Among slavery countries, the earliest were ancient Egypt along the Nile Valley, ancient Babylon and Assyria along the Euphrates and Tigris, ancient India along the Ganges River, and ancient China along the Yellow River. Among these, ancient Greece and Rome in the heart of the Mediterranean best typified the slavery society. Next we will elaborate slavery in ancient Greece.

The Greek slavery economy fully developed before the 5th century B.C. Most scholars hold that Greece was the most developed slave society in ancient times. However, the economic development of Greece was unbalanced where the slavery in different regions was distinct. In countries with a relatively long and developed slavery, slavery was divided into the Spartan type and the Athenian type. Spartan slavery had dominant agriculture and undeveloped industry and commerce, and practiced state ownership of land and employed state-owned agricultural slaves. A majority of such slaves were residents captured in war who collectively cultivated the land and turned in part of their harvest to slave owners. Athenian slavery, though still agriculture based, boasted more developed industry and commerce, had agriculture as a significant part in the commodity economy, and produced commercial crops such as grapes and olives. Significant means of production—land, slaves, and handicraft workshops—were privately owned by slave owners. The slaves were mostly traded in the market and employed in all aspects of social life. Compared to the Spartan type, the Athenian slave economy was more common and important in Greece and was more representative of the Greek slavery economy. The claim that ancient Greece was a typical slavery society is mainly in reference of the Athenian type.[10] After the Greco-Persian Wars (500 B.C. to 449 B.C.) in ancient Greece, the city-state slavery economy entered its heyday. During this time, tens of thousands of Persian prisoners of war became slaves for the Greeks and the number of slaves in city-states in Greece mushroomed. The entire free-citizen population of Athens, women and children included, numbered about 90,000. In addition, there were 365,000 slaves of both sexes and 45,000 protected persons (aliens and freedmen). There were at least 18 slaves and more than two protected persons to every adult male citizen.[11] That is to say, slaves constituted a majority of the Athenian population, with some slave owners possessing hundreds or even thousands of slaves, and medium slave owners a dozen or dozens of slaves. The use of slaves for labor was common among all production sectors in Athens and slaves were largely used to manufacture goods. Many handicraft workshops of metallurgy, pottery, shipbuilding, tanning, and weaponry manufacturing employed 20 or 30, and sometimes 100 or more slaves for manual labor. Mines employed even more slaves. For instance, 10,000–20,000 slaves worked for the Laurium silver mines. Slaves also toiled in quarries, at large farms, at public construction sites, in commercial transportation departments, and for families of slave owners. Some slave owners rented out slaves for interest. One large slave owner owned more than 1,000 slaves. Besides manual labor, rented slaves engaged in singing and dancing. Athens employed its state-owned slaves for both menial work and as police. Slaves were often brutally oppressed and exploited and traded like commodities, as often seen in Athens and Delos.

Commodity production and exchange in Athens' slavery were far more advanced than those in other slavery countries. After the Greco-Persian Wars, Athens acquired maritime hegemony, which afforded many favorable conditions for goods production in Athens, including the market, raw materials, food supplies, and a mass of slaves. Plenty of commodities produced in Athens, such as pottery, olive oil, wine, metalwork, textiles, processed farm products, and mineral products were exported to countries along the Mediterranean and the Black Sea. Athens also imported food, livestock, other agricultural products, and industrial raw materials from overseas.

The state system of Athens was a slave owner democracy. During Pericles' reign (from about 461 B.C. to 429 B.C.), the political institutions of Athens included the archon, the council of 500, the assembly, and the jury court. The assembly sat three times each month to deliberate national affairs. The council of 500 drafted bills for the assembly and managed administrative work. The archon mainly managed religious sacrifices and heard religious cases. The jury court specialized in judicial cases. Archons, senators, and jurors were selected by lot without property restrictions and served one term a year. Among the Athenian officials, only ten generals were elected by the assembly. Originally, the general was a military appointment. Due to frequent foreign wars, however, the chief general took charge of the government. For instance, Pericles was re-elected as chief general for 15 years and had long dominated the Athenian government. Engels in *The Origin of the Family, Private Property and the State* said:

> The rise of the state among the Athenians is a particularly typical example of the formation of a state; first, the process takes place in a pure form without any interference through use of violent force either from without or from within … , second, it shows a very highly developed form of state, the democratic republic, arising directly out of gentile society.[12]

The slave owner democracy was more advanced than the dictatorship of the slave owner aristocratic oligarchy and had promoted the economic and cultural development of Athens. However, it is also necessary to note that the slave owner democracy in Athens was essentially a form of dictatorship by the slave owners against the slaves. This slave owner democracy allowed as many members of the slave owning class as possible to participate directly in the rule of slaves. Lenin in *The State* said:

> In the slave owning state we had a monarchy, an aristocratic republic or even a democratic republic. In fact, the forms of government varied extremely, but their essence was always the same: The slaves enjoyed no rights and constituted an oppressed class; they were not regarded as human beings.[13]

The culture of ancient Greece was also the most developed of the slavery states. The early days of this culture witnessed Homer's epics and other poems, architecture, and pottery. From the 5th to the 4th centuries B.C., Greek culture reaped great prosperity. Athens was not only the political and economic center, but also the cultural center of Greece. From the early 5th century A.D., literature and art in Athens had gained unprecedented prosperity. The Athens' government directly managed dramatic creations and performances. Greek classical dramas were mostly operas, including both tragedies and comedies, all developed from mass festival songs and dances and ceremonies. At that time, Athens built its amphitheaters with tiered seats that could accommodate tens of thousands of spectators. Greek architecture was highly developed as well. In the satellite towns on the hills of Athens, majestic colonnaded temples were erected. Greek sculpture and arts and crafts also played an important role in the history of world art. Ancient Greek philosophy furnished a systematic worldview and incited the great debate between materialism and idealism. Democritus' spontaneous materialism and Heraclitus' Naive Dialectic played an important role in the history of philosophy and in the development of modern progressive philosophy. Lenin once called Heraclitus "one of the founders of dialectics."[14] Aristotle was an ancient encyclopedic mind, and the founder of formal logic. He studied physics, botany, zoology, and physiology and had written prolifically on history, politics, and literary theory. Scholarly achievements of ancient Greece were comprehensively summarized in Aristotle's works. Engels spoke highly of ancient Greek philosophy in *Dialectics of Nature*. He said: "In the various forms of Greek philosophy, embryos and sprouts of all subsequent views can be found. Therefore, in order to trace its formation and development history of various general principles today, the theoretical natural sciences have to go back to the Greeks too."[15] In his *Preface to A Contribution to the Critique of Political Economy*, Marx thus evaluated ancient Greek literature and art:

> Why should not the historical childhood of humanity, where it attained its most beautiful form, exert an eternal charm because it is a stage that will never recur? There are rude children and precocious children. Many of the ancient peoples belong to this category. The Greeks were normal children. The charm their art has for us does not conflict with the immature stage of the society in which it originated. On the contrary its charm is a consequence of this and is inseparably linked with the fact that the immature social conditions which gave rise, and which alone could give rise, to this art cannot recur.[16]

Marx's statement explains both the social conditions and the prosperity of ancient Greek culture among slavery states. Engels also pointed out in *Anti-Dühring*:

> It was slavery that first made possible the division of labour between agriculture and industry on a large scale, and thereby also Hellenism, the flowering of the ancient world. Without slavery, no Greek state, no Greek art and science, without slavery, no Roman Empire. But without the basis laid by Hellenism and the Roman Empire, also no modern Europe.[17]

In the Roman Republic, slavery developed greatly. Through extensive conquests and expansions, Rome captured a large amount of wealth and land, and also large numbers of slaves, which furnished conditions for the rapid development of slavery. From the 3rd to 2nd centuries B.C., Rome developed from domestic slavery to advanced labor slavery. Its military and civilian captures in the conquered areas became Rome's main feeder of slaves. In the first Punic War, Rome sold 75,000 captures as slaves. In 209 B.C., Rome captured Tarenium, and about 30,000 residents became slaves. Residents of Capua, after its capture by Rome, were sold as slaves. When Romans occupied Sardinia in 177 B.C., 80,000 people were sold as slaves, leading to plummeting prices for slaves. "Sardinian" became synonymous with cheap goods. In 167 B.C., Rome occupied Epirus, capturing 150,000 inhabitants, all sold as slaves. In addition to prisoners of war being sold as slaves, children of slaves also became slaves. These so-called family slaves were more obedient and valued by slave owners as important constituents in their slavery. During this period, the slave trade thrived with slave markets in many cities. For example, there were places to trade slaves near the Holy Path in Rome, Ephesus in Athens, Quarea on the north shore of the Adriatic Sea, Massalia at the mouth of the Lune River, as well as Cyprus and Chois that were famous slave markets. Delos was the center of the slave trade. According to Strabo, the number of slaves traded in one day was as high as 10,000.[18]

At that time, the social economy in Rome was prospering, with the use of slave labor on a large scale. Slaves were widely used in agriculture, animal husbandry, mining, as well as handicraft industry and they gradually became a major producer for Roman society. Slave labor in agriculture offered distinct advantages. Large groups of slaves were employed everywhere for country manors, vineyards, or live gardens. More slaves were needed in manors where grains were grown. The heavy labor in the mining and construction industries was done by slaves. There were 40,000 slaves in the silver mine near Nova Carthage in Spain. Handicraft industries also used slave labor. Some slaves served to manage business for their owners. At the same time, a large number of slaves were used as domestic laborers and servants. In wealthy Roman families, slaves served as gatekeepers, cooks, horse-keepers, and attendants. Skilled and educated slaves served as teachers, doctors, musicians, hairdressers, and so on. The state also employed slaves as jailers, servants, and executioners. In addition, some strong slaves were trained as gladiators, killing each other in the arena, or fighting with wild animals to entertain the Romans. Most slaves were enslaved for life. Only a few were released by their owners into freedom; however, they remained in their owners' service as former protégés.[19]

Because the slavery of ancient Rome was developed on the basis of ancient Greek slavery, the entire ancient Greek and Roman slavery was more advanced than that of Eastern countries. In some sense, not only the slavery in Athens, but also that in ancient Rome and Greece, exemplified the most developed form of slavery.

3.2.2 Models of feudal society

Ancient Greece and Rome exemplified the development of slavery. What about the feudal society? Who were the exemplars? I suppose it is China. China's ancient civilization manifested numerous features of typical feudalism.

3.2.2.1 China's feudal society was the earliest and the longest in history

There are different views on the segmentation of ancient Chinese history. If we begin from the founding of the Western Zhou Dynasty in 1066 B.C., feudalistic China had a history of about 3,000 years. If we start from the Spring and Autumn Period or the Warring States Period, that is a history of 2,200 to 2,700 years. If we count from the demise of the Western Roman Empire at the end of the 5th century A.D., to the outbreak of the British Bourgeois Revolution in the mid-17th century, the feudal society in Western Europe only had a history of 1,200 years—half the length of Chinese feudal society. Moreover, when Western Europe entered the feudal society at the end of the 5th century, China entered the Southern and Northern Dynasties after the Eastern Jin Dynasty. Through the "Silk Road," China's feudalism made worldwide contributions to the exchange between and development of Eastern and Western cultures.

3.2.2.2 China's feudal society represented the highest level of productivity and science and technology

The use of iron in Western Europe symbolizes the start of the slave society there. The use of iron in China symbolizes the start of Chinese feudalism. On the surface, Chinese feudalism may not seem as advanced as that in Western Europe. This, however, is not the case. China mastered the technology of pig iron smelting in the Spring and Autumn Period and the Warring States Period. Some countries in Europe were able to produce block iron around 1000 B.C., and Rome in its early days was occasionally able to obtain pig iron. However, such iron was discarded and cast iron was not used until the 14th century, almost 1,800 years later than China. Cast iron was produced by melting iron ore into molten iron and then casting it. Cast iron products appeared in China in the 6th century B.C. and in Europe around the 14th century after hydraulic blast equipment was invented. Cast iron technology in ancient China was an amazing achievement by being almost 2,000 years earlier than the rest of the world. China mastered ductile cast iron technology in the first half of the 5th century B.C., a highly significant achievement. As metallurgical expert Han Rufen points out:

> Ancient Chinese craftsmen invented the technology in which craftsmen cast liquid pig iron into instruments and tools, and created the annealing process to mitigate the brittleness of cast iron. Annealing provided the necessary condition for and enabled wide use of pig iron.

This important invention greatly advanced the metallurgical industry in the middle of the Warring States, and widespread use of ironware became possible. Whereas in Europe, ductile cast iron did not appear until 1700 A.D., over 2,000 years later than in China.[20] The level of metallurgical technology had a lot to do with the temperature at the time of smelting. No later than the Ming Dynasty, China had invented the coking method and improved the blowers, increasing the temperature during smelting. China's taller furnaces greatly improved the output and quality of metallurgical production. In 1713, British ironmaster Abraham Darby I knew about coking, which was about a century later than China. China used piston-type wooden bellows in the Ming Dynasty. It utilized the push of the piston to automatically open and close the valve, giving a continuous supply of large wind pressure and air volume, improving the smelting strength, expanding the capacity of the furnace, and increasing the output. This preceded the piston blowers in Europe (in the late 18th century) by at least a century.[21]

China's feudal society was also far ahead of other countries in the world in terms of water conservancy projects. During the Spring and Autumn Period, the construction of water conservancy projects in various vassal states had already reached a large scale. For example, in the late Spring and Autumn Period, Wu State built a canal, called "Han-gou" (Han Conduit), between the Yangtze River and the Huaihe River. The excavation of Han-gou facilitated transportation and agricultural irrigation. According to legend, during the reign of King Zhuang of Chu in the Spring and Autumn Period, Prime Minister Sunshu Ao built an enormous reservoir south of Shouxian County, Anhui Province. This reservoir was called Shao Bei (Peony Dam). Following the natural terrain of undulating hills, a large river dam was constructed for flood control and agricultural irrigation, a function similar to today's reservoirs. During the Warring States Period, the most famous water conservancy project was "Dujiangyan" (Dam of River Dou). There were high mountains, deep valleys, and rapids along the Minjiang River. With the river's dramatically increased water volume in summer and autumn, the Chengdu Plain was extremely prone to floods. During the reign of King Zhaoxiang of Qin, Li Bing, then governor of Shu for the state of Qin, tapped into previous experience of water control, and built the Dujiangyan water conservancy project. In the Minjiang River, west of Dujiangyan City, the Lijiangdui (Mound of Li River), which is connected to Yulei Mountain, was excavated. The dam discharged excess water into the upper reaches of Lijiangdui and divided the Minjiang River into two parts: the Pijiang River (Inner River) and the Jianjiang River (Outer River). Meanwhile, sluices were built to regulate water volume in the two rivers. Thus, the Minjiang River was diverted not only to avoid flooding, but also to facilitate shipping and irrigation. The construction of the Dujiangyan water conservancy project not only solved the flood problem of the Minjiang River, but also helped the construction of 120 canals, benefiting more than one million *mu* of farmland (one acre is about six *mu*). This great water conservancy project has been in use for more than 2,000 years and remains in use today.[22] The construction of bridges across rivers and valleys has a long history in China, the most famous of which is the Anji Bridge in Zhaozhou, Hebei Province, commonly known as Zhaozhou Bridge, designed by Li Chun, a craftsman of the Sui Dynasty. It was built in the mid-reign of Emperor Wen of Sui (591–599 A.D.). Spanning over the Tuohe River in Zhaozhou, Hebei Province, it is one of the earliest large-scale stone arch bridges. With its outstanding open-spandrel structure, exquisite architectural art, and construction techniques, the bridge has attracted worldwide attention throughout the history of bridge-building. Zhaozhou Bridge is now more than 1,300 years old. During this time, the supports of the bridge on both sides have subsided less than five centimeters. Surviving hundreds of floods and numerous earthquakes, the bridges still stands solidly over the Xiaohe River.[23] The Grand Canal, built in the Sui Dynasty, is a vast project with a length of over 2,000 km. It links together the Hai River, the Yellow River, the Huai River, the Yangtze River, and the Qiantang River, and is one of the greatest projects in world history of water conservancy. From a modern point of view, the design and construction of such a huge project, which traverses a vast and complex geography, entails advanced scientific and technical knowledge in measurement, calculation, mechanics, and hydrodynamics. It needs to solve a series of scientific and technological problems. The completion of this project reflects the ingenuity and creativity of the working people of ancient China. The Grand Canal was once the main artery of north–south transportation in China. It significantly strengthened the connection and exchanges between the North and the South, promoted the economy, and facilitated the unification of the country.

Due to the development of iron-smelting technology and the construction of water conservancy projects, ironware was widely used in agriculture and handicraft production in early feudalistic China. Iron plows popularized the use of cattle in cultivation of wasteland. This, plus the expansion of artificial irrigation, fertilization technology, and the implementation of two crops a year, greatly enhanced agricultural productivity.

Many more inventions and discoveries of science and technology in China's feudal society rank first in the world. Take the case of circumference ratio or pi as an example. Although there is evidence that the ancient Egyptians and Old Babylonians derived values such as 3.1064 and 3.125, the commonest practice in ancient civilizations was to take the ratio simply as 3. Now the ratio is 3.145926536. The first attempt at a more accurate value was seen in the Chia Liang Hu standard measure, prepared for Wang Mang by Liu Hsin in the first ten years of the 1st century A.D. From this, Chhien Pao-Tsung saw that Liu Hsin must have used a value for π of 3.154, but there is no record of how he arrived at it. The first explicit effort to obtain a more accurate figure was that of Chang Heng in about 130 A.D. In the 3rd century, Wang Fan, mathematician and astronomer of the Wu State in the Three Kingdoms Period, recalculated the value, getting 3.1555. His contemporary, Liu Huiin, of the northern Wei State, inscribed a 192-sided polygon inside a circle and derived a value of 3.14. Later, based on a 3,072-sided polygon inscribed in a circle, he derived a more accurate value of 3.14159. Then in the 5th century, Zu Chongzi and his son Zu Xuan took a leap and put China a millennium ahead in the world. They put the pi value between an "excess value" of 3.1415927 and a "deficit value" of 3.1415926. Despite the loss of the original documents of these two mathematicians, Zhao Youqin in the year 1300 A.D. used a 16,384-sided polygon inscribed in a circle. Zhao proved the high accuracy of the Zu father and son team. About 1600 A.D., Adriaan Anthoniszoon obtained a result approaching an early value derived by Zu Chongzi: 3.1415929203.[24] The compass, papermaking, gunpowder, and movable type printing are world-renowned as China's Four Great Inventions. Mao Zedong points out:

> The compass was invented in China very long ago. The art of paper-making was discovered as early as 1800 years ago. Block-printing was invented 1300 years ago, and movable type 800 years ago. The use of gunpowder was known to Chinese before the Europeans.[25]

The introduction of China's Four Great Inventions into the West has had an epic influence on European society and has become a "necessary prerequisite for the development of the bourgeoisie." Marx points out:

> Gunpowder blew away the class of knights, and the compass opened the world market and created colonies. The technology of book-printing, however, turned into a tool of Protestantism. Generally speaking, it became a medium of scientific resurge and the strongest lever for the creation of necessary conditions for intellectual development.

And all of this "omens the arrival of bourgeois society."[26]

3.2.2.3 The production relations of the feudal China were the most mature

Due to the relatively high level of productivity and science and technology, the production relations of Chinese feudal society were also superior to that of Western feudal society. Unlike manor owners' dominant possession of land in Western Europe, landlords dominated the ownership of land in China from the Qin and Han Dynasties. Under China's land ownership, free trade of land was allowed. Ownership of land depended more on economic strength than on political privileges. The family constituted the basic production unit, engaged in agriculture and household handicraft. This arrangement greatly incentivized the household producer.

In feudal society, feudal lords exploited the peasants mainly through land rent. Land rent was fundamental to and symbolic of the maturity of the feudal production relations. Labor rent, produce rent, and currency rent were the three basic forms of land rent. The successive changes in the three types of land rent reflected the different maturity levels of the production relations in feudal society.

Labor rent was the "the simplest and most primitive form of rent"[27] for feudal rent, which dominated the early days of feudal society. Under this form of ground rent, the peasants spent part of their time working on their own land and the labor products belonged to them; they spent another part of their time carrying out unpaid work for the lords through which all the labor products belonged to the feudal lords. Here, the necessary labor and surplus labor were completely separated in time and space. When peasants worked on their own land, labor enthusiasm and efficiency were relatively high. When they worked on the lords' land, labor enthusiasm and efficiency were relatively low. The feudal lords often used sticks to coerce the serfs to work.

With developed productivity, labor rent gradually yielded to the product rent. Under product rent, the landlords leased the arable land to the peasants, while the peasants regularly paid the landlords a certain amount of products, such as food, poultry, and other agricultural and sideline products. Here, the necessary labor and surplus labor of the peasants were merged together. Their labor anytime and anywhere included both the necessary labor for themselves and the surplus labor for the feudal landlords. All the labor of peasants was linked to their own vital interests, so the landlords did not have to use cruel means to coerce the peasants. Marx points out:

> Rent in kind presupposes a higher stage of civilisation for the direct producer, i.e., a higher level of development of his labour and of society in general … . The direct producer is driven rather by force of circumstances than by direct coercion, through legal enactment rather than the whip, to perform it on his own responsibility.[28]

Under product rent, farmers had certain autonomy to control their labor time. Surplus products beyond stipulated rent belonged to the farmers. Therefore, product rent enthused the farmers and promoted productivity. The transition from labor rent to product rent improved the feudal production relationship.

Product rent and labor rent as different forms of feudal land rent were products of the dominant natural economy. In the later period of the feudal society, with a better commodity economy and gradual disintegration of the natural economy, product rent gradually yielded to monetary rent. Under monetary rent, farmers had to sell a portion of their products in exchange for money, to pay for the ground rent. Monetary ground rent accelerated the commodity economy and the emergence of capitalist production relations. Marx points out: Under monetary rent,

> the character of the entire mode of production is thus more or less changed. It loses its independence, its detachment from social connection. The ratio of cost of production, which now comprises greater or lesser expenditures of money, becomes decisive; at any rate, the excess of that portion of gross

> product to be converted into money over that portion which must serve, on the one hand, as means of reproduction again, and, on the other, as means of direct subsistence, assumes a determining role.

Money rent, "is the final form, and simultaneously the form of dissolution of the type of ground-rent."

> In its further development money-rent must lead—aside from all intermediate forms, e.g., the small peasant tenant farmer—either to the transformation of land into peasants' freehold, or to the form corresponding to the capitalist mode of production, that is, to rent paid by the capitalist tenant farmer.[29]

In the feudal society of Western Europe, labor rent existed for a long time, and dominated in France before the 8th and 9th centuries. Product rent dominated after the 10th to 11th centuries when labor rent still accounted for a large proportion. In China's feudal society, labor rent existed for a relatively short period of time, while product rent existed for a long time. Product rent had always been dominant since Shang Yang's reform abolished the public field. Compared with labor rent, product rent indicated a higher level of productivity and civilization for both the producer and the society. Different forms of land rent demonstrate that China's feudal production relations were more mature and developed than those in Europe. Of course, it is undeniable that due to the long-term dominance of product rent, the natural economy was more stable, and monetary rent became difficult to form and develop, hindering the emergence and development of China's capitalist production relations. Therefore, China became a laggard in the world in the later period of feudal society.

3.2.2.4 Feudalistic China's productive forces and production relations as well as its political system surpassed those of the West

For a long time in Western Europe during the Middle Ages, feudalism fell into decay. The feudal lords were able to exercise judicial, administrative, and military powers independently in their territories, significantly thwarting economic and cultural development. It was not until the late feudal society that feudalism consolidated to produce nation states. In China, since Qin's wars of unification, the abolition of the enfeoffment system and the establishment of the prefectures and counties, the centralized absolute monarchy mostly dominated in China, despite numerous national segmentations in between. The country had unified its writing characters, currency, weights and measures, tax system, and track gauges for chariots, all of which advanced the feudal economy and culture. The centralized government controlled land accounts of the whole country through bureaucrats at all levels, and effectively maintained the feudal rule through grassroots organizations such as Bao-jia (Household System) and the Clan System. Through the indoctrination of feudal and patriarchal ideology, China's feudal system achieved further consolidation. At the same time, the centralized absolute monarchy and traditional feudal ideology suppressed the emergence and development of the commodity economy in the later period of feudal society, stunted capitalism, and prolonged feudalism in China.

3.2.2.5 Chinese feudal ideology was also highly developed

In the Spring and Autumn Period and the Warring States Period, Chinese scholarship witnessed unprecedented flowering and a constellation of talents, giving an episode called "contention among one hundred schools of thought." A great many cultural thinkers or "scholars of all schools" emerged, such as Confucius, Mencius, Xunzi, and Han Feizi. They have bequeathed a rich cultural legacy to posterity. Emperor Wu of the Han Dynasty adopted Dong Zhongshu's opinion and "banned all philosophies with sole veneration for Confucianism." This, however, did not prevent other schools of philosophy from self-expression. The government of the Han Dynasty advocated Confucianism. The establishment of the titled doctoral students in 124 B.C. was generally considered the beginning of the central educational institution called Taixue (the Imperial College in feudal China). Doctoral students were known as the students of imperial college and at their peak reached a number of 30,000. Local schools were also established gradually in all provinces and counties to give private lessons. Famous teachers attracted hundreds or thousands of disciples. The number of intellectuals increased, with expanding influence in society. They greatly promoted the feudal ideology and culture.[30] A series of classics such as *The Book of Songs*, *The Book of History*, *The Songs of Chu*, and *The Historical Records* were produced and have reached an unparalleled position in Chinese and even world history. Poems in the Tang and Song Dynasties, operas in the Yuan Dynasty, and novels in the Ming and Qing Dynasties all occupy prominent places in the history of Chinese and world culture. The Four Classics of China—*Romance of the Three Kingdoms*, *Water Margin*, *Journey to the West*, *Dream of the Red Mansion*—are highly popular with Chinese people, and have been adapted into movies, TV dramas, and cartoons.

3.2.2.6 Class relationships of Chinese feudal society were unique compared with the West

China's feudal prosperity in economy, politics, and culture were products of the landlords' economic exploitation and political oppression of the peasants. Class relations and conflicts in Chinese feudal society were more typical than in the West. Cruel exploitation and oppression of the peasants by the landlord class forced the peasants into numerous uprisings against the landlord class. The number and scale of peasant uprisings in Chinese feudal society were rare in world history. It was the peasant uprisings that propelled forward China's feudal society. Mao Zedong said in *The Chinese Revolution and the Chinese Communist Party*:

> [F]rom the uprisings of Chen Sheng, Wu Kuang, Hsiang Yu and Liu Pang in the Chin Dynasty, those of Hsinshih, Pinglin, the Red Eyebrows, the Bronze

> Horses and the Yellow Turbans in the Han Dynasty, those of Li Mi and Tou Chien-teh in the Sui Dynasty, those of Wang Hsien-chih and Huang Chao in the Tang Dynasty, those of Sung Chiang and Fang La in the Sung Dynasty, that of Chu Yuan-chang in the Yuan Dynasty, and that of Li Tzu-cheng in the Ming Dynasty, down to the uprising known as the War of the Taiping Heavenly Kingdom in the Ching Dynasty. The scale of peasant uprisings and peasant wars in Chinese history has no parallel anywhere else. The class struggles of the peasants, the peasant uprisings and peasant wars constituted the real motive force of historical development in Chinese feudal society. For each of the major peasant uprisings and wars dealt a blow to the feudal regime of the time, and hence more or less furthered the growth of the social productive forces.[31]

At the same time, we should note that peasant uprisings and wars in the feudal society of China, confined by the perceptual scope of the peasant class, merely regulated the rises and falls in China's feudal society. They not only failed to fundamentally shake or overthrow the feudal system, but actually prolonged it, serving as an important reason for longer feudalism in China than in the West.

3.2.2.7 The art of Chinese feudal society was highly developed

The art of Chinese feudal society reached a high level. For example, Chinese sculpture is closely related to Buddhism. After Buddhism was introduced in China, its practice in cave carving and Buddha statues in India also followed into China. Grottoes and Buddha statues were created in provinces such as Xinjiang, Gansu, Shanxi, Henan, Sichuan, and Shandong and passed through many dynasties such as Wei, Jin, Sui, Tang, and Song, leaving behind a treasure trove of artwork. The grotto artwork can be divided into two categories. In areas with hard rock, such as Yungang and Longmen, the main grotto artwork was stone carvings. In areas with softer rocks, such as Dunhuang Thousand-Buddha Cave and Maijishan Grottoes, the main works of art were murals and clay sculptures. Among these, the Dunhuang, Yungang, and Longmen Grottoes are the most celebrated.[32]

3.2.3 An analysis of Melotti's mistake

Some Chinese and foreign scholars not only deny China's feudalism as a typical example of feudal society in world history with the highest level of development, but also deny that China has experienced the feudal society. They think China was of a typical "Asiatic mode of production," which remained dominant in China from the dissolution of the primitive commune till China's degeneration into a semi-colony to Western powers. Professor Umberto Melotti of the Art Institute of Milan in Italy holds this view in his book *Marx and the Third World*. He believes that the "Asiatic mode of production" or "Asian society" has three basic characteristics:

> First, there is no land private ownership. To say the least, the land belongs to the country. Second, the foundation of Asian society is the village community, and each village community is self-sufficient through the close integration of agriculture and family handcrafts. Third, centralization plays a dominant role.[33]

This view does not conform to China's historical facts.

First, the three characteristics mentioned above are nonexistent in any stage of Chinese feudal society. It was only in the Western Zhou Dynasty that some but not all of the three characteristics were identifiable. It would be an exaggeration to claim that, between the dissolution of Chinese primitive communities and the time prior to the Opium War by foreign imperialist invasion, China embodied the above three characteristics simultaneously. As known to us, in the mid-11th century B.C. after Western Zhou had overthrown the Shang Dynasty, the Kings of Zhou, based on the patriarchal and hierarchical clan system, distributed land and people to their descendants, royal relatives, and meritorious statesmen through the "awards of people and land." Recipients were called "zhuhou," or seigneurs, classified into five peerages of "Gong, Hou, Bo, Zi, and Nan," similar to the British nobility peerages of "Duke, Marquis, Earl, Viscount, and Baron." These seigneurs in turn distributed their awarded land and people to their own descendants and subjects. This multi-layered enfeoffment formed a pagoda-like hierarchy. However, land ownership belonged to the Zhou Kings, seen as representative of the state, while seigneurs of all levels only enjoyed tenure and distribution of land. Similarly, farmers were only entitled to use the land of their share. This is recorded in the chapter "Discourses of Jin" in the book *Discourses of the States*, "seigneurs feed on contributions, high officials on their enfeoffment, low officials on their land, and commoners on their own labor."

The earliest discussion about the land system in the Western Zhou Dynasty came from Mencius. There was a detailed description of the land system in the Western Zhou Dynasty in the chapter of "Teng Wen Gong" (Lord Teng Wen) of the book *Mencius*:

> In the fields of a district, those who belong to the same nine squares render all friendly offices to one another in their going out and coming in, aid one another in keeping watch and ward, and sustain one another in sickness. Thus the people are brought to live in affection and harmony. A square lî covers nine squares of land, which nine squares contain nine hundred mâu. The central square is the public field, and eight families, each having its private hundred mâu, cultivate in common the public field. And not till the public work is finished, may they presume to attend to their private affairs.

It can be inferred here that the fundamental unit of social organization in Western Zhou was the rural community. Inside one rural community, the chief landlord would enjoy tenure and distribution rights of all the farmland, which was divided into smaller squares for each farmer to cultivate. The "private fields" in "eight families, each having its private hundred mâu (of fields)" were equivalent to an "allotment" in Western European and Russian rural communities. The regular redistribution of "private fields," every one or two or three years, was based on the fertility of the farming fields. The remainder of the field, owned by the chief landlord, was called the "public field," equivalent to "common land" in Western Europe. The "public field" was the common tillage by the farmers. Farmers would not attend to their affairs in the "private fields" until they had cultivated the "public field"—"not till the public work is finished, may they presume to attend to their private affairs," as in the words of Mencius. This reflects the fact that exploitation was done in labor rent and the class antagonism was between the landlords and the peasants. The endeavors of Mencius to beautify and praise this land system reflected his relatively conservative political standpoint.

At the end of the Zhou Dynasty, especially during the Spring and Autumn Period, land ownership changed due to agricultural development. The change occurred in two manners, one being that the tenure of land decreased gradually for all levels of aristocrats. As the aristocrats gained increasing power, the King of Zhou became less controlling. All levels of aristocrats—seigneurs, ministers, high and low officials—gradually usurped as their own the land entitled to them by the Zhou King. This consequently made them aristocratic landlords. The second manner of change was the enhancement of private ownership of "private fields," leading to sharp class antagonism between the landlords and the farmers as a result of a great many self-managing peasants losing their land.

The private ownership of land in China was formed and established nationwide during the time between the Warring States and Emperor Qin's unification of the six states into one empire. The Shang Yang reforms in the Qin State was a reform of the land system, in which the legitimacy of the private ownership of land was acknowledged, thus advancing the private ownership of land. With increasing private ownership of land, land annexation worsened as a problem, widening the gap between rich and poor. Just as Sima Qian said, "Strife reigned during the Warring States when deception goes before virtue and wealth before generosity. The affluent amassed vast wealth while the impoverished fed on chaffs." Dong Zhongshu corroborated, "Qin revised its imperial system through the Shang Yang reforms. Gridded land plots were abolished and allowed for free trade. Land of the rich extended far while that of the poor was barely enough to plant one's feet." After the unification of China by Emperor Qin, over 120,000 affluent households were relocated to the Xianyang area, which demonstrated the severity of land annexation and the huge gap between the rich and the poor. Hereby the private ownership of land obtained legitimacy in a unified nation and marked the establishment of landlord private ownership of land.[34]

Three forms of land ownership existed after the Qin and Han Dynasties: Landlord private ownership, state land ownership, and freeholders' ownership of small land. Among the three, landlord private ownership held a dominant status, which is generally agreed among academics and a proposition congruent with historical reality. Therefore, it contradicts China's historical reality to contend that land ownership in China has been public from the disintegration of primitive communities to the time prior to the Opium War.

One theoretical root of the claim that there was no private ownership of land in China is the failure to recognize the ownership of land as an objective economic fact, a fact belonging to the realm of production relations. Rather, this claim views land ownership as a matter of sovereignty and legality. Indeed, feudal states exercised control over land. State laws acknowledged aristocratic landlords' tenure but not ownership of land. Yet legality did not equate to actuality. In actuality, aristocratic landlords held ownership as well as tenure of their land, as evinced by the fact that they could sell their cropland.

The opinion that there has never been private ownership of land in Chinese history sometimes finds its support in Bei Shan's chapter the "Minor Odes of the Kingdom" in the book *The Book of Songs*, "Under the wide heaven, all is the king's land. Within the sea-boundaries of the land, all are the king's servants." Such support, however, has no validity, for several reasons. First, the quote describes the situation in Western Zhou and may not apply to China's entire feudal society up to the time prior to the Opium War. Second, the quote addresses sovereign state territory instead of land ownership. State territory differs from state-owned land. The former delineates the boundary of the state as determined by history; the latter, land owned by the state. Every country exercises sovereignty over its territory, including levying taxes on the residents. Since ancient people saw the emperor as the representative of the state, namely "his majesty is the state," state territory was seen as the land of the emperor, the residents on it the subjects. The quote is an exact description of state territory and sovereignty. The land, however, could be owned by the state but could also be owned privately. Sovereignty of land and ownership of land are two different concepts.

Second, the claim that village communities have always been the foundation for Asiatic societies does not agree with historical facts. To some extent, village communities did exist in Chinese and European feudal societies. They have two distinct features. The first is the duality of public and private land ownership. The second is the freedom and equality espoused within the village community. The village communities fulfilled dual functions in feudalism—they were the basic social unit whereby the landlords exploited and oppressed the peasants and whereby the latter fought against the former. The village community in China was rather short-lived. Scholars generally accept that the village community existed in Western Zhou and the Spring and Autumn periods but dissolved upon entering into feudalism. Its dissolution may be traced back to the 7th or 4th century B.C. The Shang Yang reforms abolished the gridded land plots and allowed free trade and cultivation of cropland. That marked the official dissolution of the village community. After the Qin and Han Dynasties, vestiges of the village community were barely visible in isolated aspects of society. However, in Europe, especially among Germanics and Slavs, village communities enjoyed significant longevity. The Mark commune served as the foundation for the whole medieval social organization.[35]

Third, an important reason for Umberto Melotti's argument that China is a typical Asiatic society is that Chinese feudal society was an absolute centralized monarchy. This is invalid because the centralized absolute monarchy in China, as a form of government, did not share inherent and necessary connection with the "Asiatic production mode" (the village community and public ownership in Melotti's reference). Such monarchy could be built on slavery or on feudalism and is found both in Asia and in Europe. Feudalism in Europe was for a long time in a state of segmentation, although in its later years such as in France, there emerged a centralized monarchy. The foundations of the centralized absolute monarchy in Chinese feudal society were not the village community or public ownership of land. As mentioned before, the history of the political system in Chinese feudal society indicates that the state power of a centralized absolute monarchy built on landlord private ownership of land and small-scale peasant production mode was much consolidated and more powerful than that built on the village community and public ownership of land.

This is the case not only for China but also for Europe. Just as Marx said in his article "The Eighteenth Brumaire of Louis Bonaparte," a centralized absolute monarchy was generated in the collapse of feudalism in France with a foundation on small peasants. He added,

> The executive power with its enormous bureaucratic and military organization, with its wide-ranging and ingenious state machinery, with a host of officials numbering half a million, besides an army of another half million—this terrifying parasitic body which enmeshes the body of French society and chokes all its pores sprang up in the time of the absolute monarchy, with the decay of the feudal system which it had helped to hasten … . The first French Revolution, with its task of breaking all separate local, territorial, urban, and provincial powers in order to create the civil unity of the nation, was bound to develop what the monarchy had begun, centralization, but at the same time the limits, the attributes, and the agents of the governmental power. Napoleon completed this state machinery.

After going through the Legitimate Monarchy, the July Monarchy, and the parliamentary republic, and after the French coup d'état of Louis Bonaparte on December 2, 1851, France established the centralized second republic, which is

> not suspended in the air. Bonaparte represented a class, and the most numerous class of French society at that, the small-holding peasants … . Just as the Bourbons were the dynasty of the big landed property and the Orleans the dynasty of money, so the Bonapartes are the dynasty of the peasants, that is, the French masses. The chosen of the peasantry is not the Bonaparte who submitted to the bourgeois parliament but the Bonaparte who dismissed the bourgeois parliament.[36]

Twenty years later, Marx concluded about the lessons and experience of the Paris Commune Revolution in his work *The Civil War in France* and said,

> The centralized state power, with its ubiquitous organs of standing army, police, bureaucracy, clergy, and judicature—organs wrought after the plan

> of a systematic and hierarchic division of labor—originates from the days of absolute monarchy, serving nascent middle class society as a mighty weapon in its struggle against feudalism. Still, its development remained clogged by all manner of medieval rubbish, seignorial rights, local privileges, municipal and guild monopolies, and provincial constitutions. The gigantic broom of the French Revolution of the 18th century swept away all these relics of bygone times, thus clearing simultaneously the social soil of its last hinderances to the superstructure of the modern state edifice raised under the First Empire, itself the offspring of the coalition wars of old semi-feudal Europe against modern France.

After that, there were the Legitimate Monarchy, the July Monarchy, and the parliamentary republic, till the establishment of the second empire.

> In reality, it was the only form of government possible at a time when the bourgeoisie had already lost, and the working class had not yet acquired, the faculty of ruling the nation. It was acclaimed throughout the world as the savior of society. Under its sway, bourgeois society, freed from political cares, attained a development unexpected even by itself … . Imperialism is, at the same time, the most prostitute and the ultimate form of the state power which nascent middle class society had commenced to elaborate as a means of its own emancipation from feudalism, and which full-grown bourgeois society had finally transformed into a means for the enslavement of labor by capital.[37]

Marx's above statements demonstrate that: (1) The French absolute monarchy was generated in the decay of feudalism and completed during the French Empire, which served as a powerful weapon for the emerging bourgeoisie against feudalism. (2) After establishment of the bourgeois ruling, especially during the second French Republic, the absolute monarchy became the bourgeoisie's tool to oppress the proletariat. (3) The superstructure of the French centralized monarchy was not suspended in the air but rooted in the mass of small-holding peasants.

A comparison of Asia and Europe indicates that the absolute monarchy is not exclusive to China or even Asia. In the decay of feudalism, the French absolute monarchy was generated and served as a powerful weapon for the emerging bourgeoisie not only to fight against feudalism, but also to oppress the proletariat. This again demonstrates that there is no inherent and necessary connection between (1) the absolute monarchy and (2) the village community and public ownership of land. During the emergence, development, and consolidation of the French absolute monarchy, village communities were either nonexistent or in further decay.

Fourth, Melotti denied the antagonism between slave owners and slaves and between feudal landlords and peasants. He argued that the actual exploiting class, in a typical Asiatic society like China, was the "bureaucratic group." He defamed modern Chinese socialism as a "bureaucratic collectivism" built on the "Asiatic production mode" and defamed the people's democratic dictatorship as a country of "bureaucratic collectivism." These statements contradict the Marxian concept of state and China's historical facts. According to Marx's conception, the state is a product and manifestation of irreconcilable class antagonism, an organ for the oppression of one class by another. State officials, from the highest to the lowest, are political representatives of the ruling class. They are not and will not make an independent class. In the slavery society of China, the basic classes opposing each other were slave owners and slaves. In order to protect their own economic benefits and to suppress the revolts of slaves, slave owners established their own state and served as their own representatives. After the Spring and Autumn Period, the emerging class of landlords overthrew the declining ruling of slave owners, to establish a state power of the feudal landlord class. Between the Qin and Han Dynasties and the Qing Dynasty, the body of political officials continued to expand with an enhanced absolute monarchy. However, officials of all dynasties, levels, and backgrounds, by nature of their class, were political representatives of the feudal landlords. They were not and could not constitute an independent social class. True, the central authority would sometimes restrict and suppress certain segments of the feudal landlords. For instance, in the interest of large landlords, the central authority may restrict and suppress the small landlords. Reversely, it may go against the large landlords to prevent bankruptcy of the small landlords. But this is for the protection of the landlords as an entire class and does not indicate that the bureaucrat would form its own class independent of the landlords. For the purpose of distorting the class relations in ancient China, Melotti distorted the exploitation method in feudalistic China. He believes that rent and tax in China have always been one, and that no land rent exists outside taxation. This goes against China's true history. As explained before, there existed three forms of land ownerships in China, namely ownership by landlords, by the state, and by smallholders. The integrated tax and rent only applied to state-owned land in the form of wasteland reclamation and cultivation. In landlord ownership, peasants paid rent to their landlords, who then paid taxes to the state. As for the smallholders, they paid taxes to the state.

Some scholars deny China's feudal society as typical because they use the feudal system of Western Europe as the model, which, in their view, is characterized by serfdom, manorial ownership, and political pluralism. Since China did not bear above three characteristics, they argue, China never went through a feudal society. This is undeniably Eurocentrism misapplied to the study of ancient Chinese history.

In my opinion, it is unscientific to use the above three characteristics to describe the feudal society, as they were simply not applicable to feudalism in Eastern countries. In addition, even in the feudalism of Western Europe which the cited scholars consider as the model of feudalism, the three characteristics have not been fully realized.

First of all, let's investigate the social serfdom and manorialism. Recent historical studies in the world indicate that, after the completion of feudalization in Western Europe, there were still a large number of freeholding peasants independent of the manor. These peasants were constantly appropriated by manor owners who expropriated the former's land and freedom. Yet these peasants kept coming up and remained at about a constant number. The estate of Mâcon, studied by the French historian Georges Duby, was a typical feudalized area north of Loire. At Varanges, a little hamlet next to Cluny, 47 freeholders were counted in the second half of the 10th century, some of whom tried to expand the land in their holding. One couple, for instance, purchased 11 small parcels of land totaling about an acre at a price of 28 sous. Land ownership was only reflected in manorial records, which excluded the freeholding peasants. As a result, freeholding peasants were reckoned to be a rather low number in feudalistic Western Europe. It is even more improbable that after its feudalism, Western Europe only practiced manorial management of land. Many manors were a part of the village while the rest independently belonged to freeholding peasants. These peasants were exploited by the feudal system. They had to pay the tithe to the church on the one hand, and on the other hand were exploited by the feudal lords under the pretext of banned use of land. However, freeholders, unlike serfs, were allowed to own their land. According to historian Latouche, the Frankish Kingdom covered an area of 1.5 million square kilometers, among which the property of religious nobility amounted to only a few million hectares, making up only a small part; the rest of the land was forests, wasteland, and cropland of independent landowners. There were not many manors.[38]

Second, let's look into the issue of political pluralism. Political pluralism or political fragmentation was a product of Western Europe under special historical conditions, rather than a phenomenon throughout the whole feudal society of Western Europe. Political pluralism in Western Europe was most pronounced in early feudalism. After conquering the Roman Empire, Germans established several feudal countries in Western Europe between the 5th and the 6th centuries. Therefore, political pluralism had already existed in the very beginning, and was not constructed by "feudalization" later. For that matter, it cannot be used as a manifestation of "feudalization." Since the mid-12th century, the feudal monarchy became stronger in Western Europe. During the reign of Philip II (1180–1223 A.D.), the royal family very much expanded its territories in France. During the reign of Louis IX (1226–1276 A.D.), the kingship was strengthened through judicial, monetary, and military reforms. During the reign of Philip IV (1285–1314 A.D.), the royal territory included most of the land in France. France's first Estates General in 1302 showed that, through the strengthening of the kingship, the feudal lord system had evolved from the past fragmentation to a central stratified monarchy (which was a stage of the centralized monarchy). There was also a tendency for England to move from fragmentation to unification. England split into seven small countries from the 7th to the 9th centuries, i.e., in the early stage of the feudal society. Later, in their struggle against the Normans, who invaded northeastern England, the seven countries gradually became united. During the reign of Henry II (1133–1189 A.D.), the royal family fought against big feudal lords, deprived the latter's political power and dismantled more than 300 castles built during the civil war, greatly strengthening the kingship through judicial and military reforms. These facts show that the feudal society in Western Europe, in its due course, had witnessed the change from political fragmentation to political unity and the strengthening of feudal monarchy.[39] Indeed, compared with the feudal society in Western Europe, China's feudal society had a longer period of political unification. The centralized monarchy of China had been established earlier with much stronger power; however, Western Europe witnessed a longer period of political fragmentation, and its centralized monarchy was much weaker and was established much later than China. However, political unification or fragmentation is not a yardstick to assess whether a society is feudalistic. In the long history of China's feudalism, there had been several nationwide fragmentations, such as the Three Kingdoms, the Five Dynasties, and Ten Kingdoms, as well as the Sixteen Kingdoms. Can we then claim that China was a feudal society only when it was politically fragmented, but wasn't a feudal society when it became united?

In conclusion, it is unscientific to regard social serfdom, manorialism, and political pluralism as the basic features of feudal society. If we take these three as the yardstick, neither China nor Western Europe would ever have gone through feudalism. This would negate the existence of feudal society from the entirety of human history.

3.3 Germany's direct transition from the primitive society to feudal society

In the discussion of the "Asiatic mode of production," some scholars deny the theory of five social forms in successive replacement, on the ground that the Germans did not have a separate slave society after the disintegration of the primitive commune, but directly transitioned to the feudal society. These scholars then believe that the primitive society may be succeeded by either the slave society or the feudal society; therefore, the slave society and the feudal society could coexist simultaneously as parallel social forms. These scholars contend, wrongly, that the primitive society, the slave society, and the feudal society do not represent a chronology of successive replacement.

First, during the decay of the Germanic primitive society, the first form of exploitation was slavery, with the first class division between slave owners and slaves. The main sources of slaves for Germans were prisoners of war, especially women and children captured during the war. At the end of the 1st century B.C., Germans already began to keep slaves. Later, their victories gave them a larger number of prisoners of war. After the establishment of the Frankish Kingdom at the end of the 5th century, the number of slaves increased greatly. The prisoners of war, plus the surviving slaves of the Western Roman Empire, provided a body of slaves much greater than that in the late Roman Empire. Germanic slavery was as cruel as Roman slavery. The Germanic slave owners also regarded slaves as their own private property that could be purchased or sold, gifted or slaughtered at will. As early as the Tacitus era, the Germans were prone to kill slaves, incited more by anger than by disciplinarian purposes. They killed slaves as if killing an enemy without being punished. The laws of the Frankish Kingdom stipulated that: The whip for torturing slaves must not be thinner than the pinkie. The Laws of Ine, one of the early Anglo-Saxon codes, stipulated that: When paying the wergild, if necessary, every hundred shillings can be replaced by a slave, a chain armor and a sword.[40] This evinces the extremely low status of slaves.

Since slavery was created during the disintegration of the primitive communes of the Germans, and the number of slaves increased in a short time after the Germans conquered the Roman Empire, why didn't the Germans continue to develop slavery after conquering the Roman Empire to enter the slave society, but instead directly entered into the feudal society instead? We believe that, under the then historical conditions, due to the development of productive forces, slavery in the whole world had been weakened. Meanwhile, the new feudal production relations had been bred within the Roman Empire. For that matter, the Germans had to adapt to the objective requirements of the developed productive forces and the trend of the entire world. They had to develop and adapt to the already existing feudal production relations on the ruins of the Roman Empire. Consequently, they could have leaped over the slave society and directly transition to the feudal society. The following will describe the birth of feudalism in the late Roman Empire.

Second, the serfdom of the Middle Ages in Europe was derived from the colonus system of the Roman Empire. The colonus system appeared as early as the end of the Roman Republic or the 1st century B.C. The coloni originally referred to the tenant farmers, whose composition and status later changed significantly. In the second half of the 2nd century A.D., due to improved production tools and the constant revolt of slaves, the latifundia based on slave labor became increasingly unprofitable, while the small-scale operation suitable for the developed productivity became more favorable to slave owners. At that time, many latifundium owners, the large landowners later, often divided their land into small pieces and rented them to former slaves for cultivation. Slaves who rented the land became coloni and served as the main source of coloni. In addition, the coloni also came from Germanic captives and immigrants. From late 2nd century to the 3rd century, the slave owners of the Roman Empire no longer treated prisoners of war as slaves but turned them into coloni. Germanic immigrants were often placed in sparsely populated or deserted areas. Another source of coloni was poor free peasants who could not pay the heavy taxes and were unable to protect themselves. Consequently, they had to turn to protection by big landlords and thus became coloni. Sometimes even all the free peasants in an entire village were sheltered by large landowners.

Generally, coloni rented a piece of land from the owner and paid rent to the owner. The rent was paid initially by money, but later by materials plus a certain amount of labor. The coloni also had to pay the state tax, usually collected by the owner and then sent to the government. In addition, the coloni were obligated to serve in the army. According to Roman laws, coloni were free men. However, due to debts and other reasons, they were actually tied to the owner's land and could even be sold or transferred with the land. Coloni's ownership of production tools varied. Some of them had a certain degree of ownership, while others had nothing. Even if they owned their property, they may not transfer it without their owner's permission. The exploitation and oppression suffered by coloni was heavy, but not as bad as for the slaves. Coloni were allowed to get married. When they had a family with a weak independent economy, the quality of their labor was directly related to their own vital interests, leading to improved enthusiasm in production. This in turn promoted the adoption of advanced production tools and technologies and consequently boosted productivity. In short, the class status and attributes of coloni were different from that of slaves, but similar to that of serfs in the Middle Ages.[41]

In his *The Origin of the Family, Private Property and the State*, Engels discussed the historical necessity and the emergence of the coloni system and their class attributes. He said:

> Agriculture, always the decisive branch of production throughout the ancient world, was now more so than ever. In Italy, the enormous estates (latifundia) which, since the end of the republic, occupied almost the whole country, had been exploited in two different ways. They had been used either as pastures, the population being displaced by sheep and cattle, which could be tended by a few slaves, or as country estates (villae), where large-scale horticulture was carried on with masses of slaves, partly as a luxury for the owner, partly for sale in the town markets. The great grazing farms had kept going and had probably even extended; the country estates and their gardens had been ruined through the impoverishment of their owners and the decay of the towns. The system of latifundia run by slave labor no longer paid; but at that time no other form of large-scale agriculture was possible. Small production had again become the only profitable form. One country estate after another was cut up into small lots, which were handed over either to tenants, who paid a fixed sum and had hereditary rights, or to partiarii, stewards rather than tenants, who received a sixth or even only a ninth of the year's product in return for their labor. For the most part, however, these small lots of land were given out to coloni, who paid for them a definite yearly amount, were tied to the soil and could be sold together with their lot. True, they were not slaves, but neither were they free; they could not marry free persons, and their marriages with one another were not regarded as full marriages, but, like those of slaves, as mere concubinage (contubernium). They were the forerunners of the medieval serfs.[42]

The large landowners, aka owners of the coloni, who mainly exploited coloni, gradually changed from the original slave owners to the feudal lords by changing their way of exploitation. In other words, the large landowners or the owners of coloni acted as the would-be feudal lords, the predecessor to the medieval feudal lords. From the perspective of development trends, although large landlords or owners of coloni still used slave labor, this kind of labor was mainly used for household duties and handicrafts, as well as work such as grape planting and flower growing, rather than for large-scale farming. Slave labor was only a supplement to the economy supported by the coloni system and did not affect the class attribute of the large landowners or the owners of coloni. This phenomenon, i.e., keeping part of the slave labor, existed not only in the economy supported by the coloni system, which served as the transition between slavery to feudalism, but also in the feudal society, for it was not completely abolished after the establishment of feudalism. For example, in the land survey inventory compiled by King William I of England in 1086, the number of slaves took up about 9% of the total population of England. In human history, it's been rather common for a certain exploiting class to use a combination of primary and secondary methods of exploitation. The large landowners or coloni owners cannot be regarded as slaveholders simply because of their supplementary use of exploitation methods seen in a slavery society.

In summary, in the context of villeinage, the latifundia owners or the coloni owners possessed production materials, but did not have direct possession of the coloni or the direct producers; land management combined large-scale land ownership and small-scale peasant economy; and the main exploitation method was that the latifundia owners or the coloni owners exploited the surplus labor of the coloni in the form of land rent. These characteristics were similar to those of the feudal system. Therefore, villeinage was feudalistic.

The social role of villeinage was two-fold. On the one hand, due to varied reasons—the slavery crisis in Rome, the unprofitability and difficulty of large-scale slavery, and the freeholders' dislike of labor—the coloni became the main agricultural producers in time and provided Roman society with materials for their survival. In this regard, the emergence of villeinage inhibited the pernicious consequences of the slavery crisis in Rome. On the other hand, due to the emergence and continuous development of villeinage, the latifundia owners or the coloni owners developed a style of their own. They engaged mainly in agriculture and concurrently in handicrafts. Their products were mainly for their own needs and those of the coloni and slaves they possessed. These products were not sold on the market. This gave a self-sufficient natural economic system. In politics, the latifundia owners or the coloni owners controlled the administrative, judicial, taxation, and other powers within their latifundia, and were equipped with private military and prisons. They completely ignored the authority of the Roman Empire and even refused the officials of the Roman Empire to enter their latifundia. Such self-contained, self-ruled, and separatist latifundia were quite similar to the feudal territory in the Medieval Ages, and greatly weakened the power of the Roman Empire and accelerated the disintegration of Roman slavery. Villeinage was a major internal force behind the transition from slavery to feudalism in Rome. And the invasion by the Germans only accelerated the collapse of slavery and the emergence of feudalism. Without the Germans' conquest, the Western Roman Empire would have been able to escape the predicament of the slavery crisis and gradually transition to the feudal society from villeinage.[43]

Third, the Western Roman Empire collapsed in 476 A.D., which historians generally use to mark the change of Western European slave society into feudal society. Then, what was the driving force behind this change? I contend that this driving force can be divided into an internal one and an external one.

The internal force refers to factors within the Roman Empire that led to the collapse of slavery and the formation of feudalism. There are mainly three factors here:

First, the new productive forces were the most profound material basis that precipitated the collapse of Roman slavery and the establishment of feudalism. In *The Origin of the Family, Private Property and the State*, Engels said:

> Social conditions were no less desperate. Already in the last years of the republic the policy of Roman rule had been ruthlessly to exploit the provinces; the empire, far from abolishing this exploitation, had organized it. The more the empire declined, the higher rose the taxes and levies, the more shamelessly the officials robbed and extorted. The Romans had always been too occupied in ruling other nations to become proficient in trade and industry; it was only as usurers that they beat all who came before or after. What commerce had already existed and still survived was now ruined by official extortion; it struggled on only in the eastern, Greek part of the empire, which lies outside the present study. General impoverishment; decline of commerce, handicrafts and art; fall in the population; decay of the towns; relapse of agriculture to a lower level—such was the final result of Roman world rule.

The scholarly community has different understandings of Engels' discussions. Some hold that Engels talks about the absolute backwardness of the productive forces at the end of the Roman Empire, which seemed to lag behind the general productivity in the entire slave society. Therefore, they conclude that the feudal society was established based on a level of productivity below that of a slave society. They even deny the successive transformation between the slave society and the feudal society.

This point of view is incorrect, or at least not comprehensive. What Engels is discussing here is not the absolute backwardness of the productive forces in the late Roman Empire, but the decaying economic and political system of slavery that seriously hindered and damaged development of the productive forces. In fact, from a general view, the productive forces of the late Roman Empire were not only much higher than those of the primitive society, but also higher than the general development level of the slave society. During the Roman slavery crisis, production technology also developed slowly.[44] For example, water mills which were rarely used before the 4th century, were promoted in the 4th century; agricultural technology and division of labor also developed. *The Work of Farming* by Palladius in the 4th century recorded that there were skilled excavation workers, reapers, grape growers, and rare bird breeding workers in agriculture at that time; meanwhile winemaking and oil extraction also developed slowly. At the end of the 4th century, there were 115 cities in the Gaul area. At that time, the political situation was turbulent, and war continued everywhere. The residents built high walls around cities, turning cities into something like castles. But they remained a hub for business and industry. After the 3rd century, business exchanges in Spain, Narbonne (at the mouth of the Tiber River in Italy), Rome, Egypt, and Syria had not been interrupted. From the 4th to the 5th centuries, local markets and local business exchanges in various provinces still existed. The slavery economy in England, which started late, reached its heyday from the 3rd to the 4th centuries. It is the level of productive forces created by Roman slavery that furnished the deepest material basis for the burial of slavery.[45]

Not only historical facts, but also the law that relations of production must correspond to the nature of productive forces dictate that the demise of old relations of production and the establishment of new relations of production need a foundation higher than the general development level of the productive forces of the former social formation. And when the old relations of production seriously hindered or even damaged the development of the productive forces, new relations of production needed to emerge. On the one hand, without a foundation of better productivity, the old relations of production will not perish, and the new ones won't emerge. On the other hand, if the old relations of production did not hinder the development of the productive forces, no new production relations would arise to replace the old. If productivity that is hindered and damaged by old production relations is considered the same as low productivity itself, the inevitable conclusion would be: The productivity as based on the production relations of any society in its late stage would be lower than that of the previous social form. Such a conclusion not only violates historical facts, but also fundamentally denies the laws that the relations of production must correspond to the nature of productive forces. The productivity level of any social form must be examined through the entire development of this social form. It is the long-term accumulation of the productive forces in Roman slavery that formed the fundamental driving force for breaking through the production relations of slavery. Although this kind of productive forces were seriously damaged in the later part of the slave society, it was still, in general, higher than the average productivity of the slave society, so that the higher social form of feudalism can possibly emerge on an enhanced productivity level.

Second, the feudal forces that spontaneously formed within the Roman society (i.e., villeinage) were the new social and economic forces that compelled the collapse of slavery and the formation of the feudal society. This has been explained previously and won't be repeated here.

Finally, the class struggle of slaves against the slave owners was one of the direct forces driving the demise of the slave society. It is undisputed that the slave class, due to its limitations, did not represent a new mode of production, and could not ultimately eliminate slavery and establish a feudal system. However, the historical role of the class struggle of the slave class against the slave owner class must not be underestimated and denied. Slave uprisings and riots played a significant role in the demise of the Western Roman Empire. In 238 A.D., slaves and coloni broke out in an uprising in Algeria in North Africa; in 236 A.D, slaves in Sicily set off a revolutionary climax; and in 273 A.D., a coin-minters' riot broke out in the city of Rome. Slaves, coloni, and peasants in Gaul initiated the Bagaudic movement in the 370s A.D. In the mid-4th century A.D., the Bagaudic movement showed a new upsurge and expanded from Gaul to Spain. In the 4th century A.D., slaves, coloni, and peasants waged various fights against slave owners in North Africa, dealing a severe blow upon the reactionary rule of the slave owner class and created the necessary conditions for the new feudal system to replace the old slavery system. The Germanic conquest of Rome was also supported by Roman slaves in some areas.

Our arguments presented so far have demonstrated the internal forces driving the collapse of the Roman slave society and the establishment of a feudal society. With such forces, the Roman Empire would perish, and the feudal society would have emerged even without the invasion by the Germans.

So, can we deny the role of the Germanic conquest? Certainly not. The Germanic conquest, an external driving force, not only accelerated the demise of Roman slavery and the establishment of the new feudalism, but also gave the feudal system of Western Europe certain characteristics associated with the Germans.

The land system pursued by the Germanic commune had a great influence on the feudal manorial economy in Western Europe. The Germanic Mark commune pursued a land system that combined the public land system, the allotment system, and the open-field system. The arable land of the Mark commune was divided into small parcels, which were distributed to the farmers in regular rotation. Out of this came the allotment system in Western European feudal manors. Each parcel of arable land of the Mark commune, when fallow, was used as common pasture. On land plowed that year, farmers had to dismantle their fences to turn it into public pasture after the harvest and before the next seeding. This was called the open-field system. The system remained popular in feudal manors in Western Europe. In the Mark commune, uncultivated land, water surface, forests, pastures, wastelands, swamps, rivers, and lakes were owned by the commune and used by all members. This was called the common land system. In feudal manors in Western Europe, this kind of common land system remained for a long time. In *The German Ideology*, Marx and Engels point out:

> In contrast to Greece and Rome, feudal development at the outset, therefore, extends over a much wider territory, prepared by the Roman conquests and the spread of agriculture at first associated with it. The last centuries of the declining Roman Empire and its conquest by the barbarians destroyed a number of productive forces; agriculture had declined, industry had decayed for want of a market, trade had died out or been violently suspended, the rural and urban population had decreased. From these conditions and the mode of organisation of the conquest determined by them, feudal property developed under the influence of the Germanic military constitution.[46]

The Germanics used a favorable military system. That is, it allowed the military chiefs to privately recruit their own soldiers or guards, who were nothing but mercenaries for war bounty. These recruits were turned into the core of battle commanders. During the expedition to Rome, the Germanic kings distributed large pieces of captured land to their guards according to their ranks, resulting in a hierarchy of Germanic landlords. Later, facilitated by the productivity of Rome, the Germanic favorable military system and the feudal land ownership jointly promoted the formation of Western European feudal hierarchy.

Fourth, it can be seen from the above three points that the direct transition of Germans from primitive society to feudal society did not negate the succession from slave society to feudal society.

First of all, the direct transition of Germans from primitive society to feudal society was achieved under specific historical conditions. Any social form is created and developed in a certain historical era. Slavery at the time was disintegrating and becoming outmoded around the world. Feudalism was established in some Eastern countries and was in embryo in Western Europe. Under such historical conditions, Germans were able to establish feudalism on the ruins of Roman slavery, which would have been impossible before. Let us review the history of the contact between Germans and Romans. By the late 2nd century B.C., Germans moved south across the Rhine and fought with the Romans many times. In the second half of the 2nd century A.D., Germans crossed the Danube River and entered the fringes of Rome. In the 3rd century A.D., Germans broke through Rome's defenses along the Rhine and penetrated into Roman territory. Small-scale conflicts between Germans and Romans were constant. But because Romans still maintained some national strength, slavery had not yet dissolved and feudalism had not emerged or was still weak. Germans were not strong enough to destroy Rome and much less to establish feudalism in Rome. Only when Rome's slavery had dissolved, its national power had declined, and the embryo of feudalism emerged and was nurtured, could Germans conquer Rome and establish a feudal system on the ruins of Roman slavery. This was precisely how the slave society transformed into the feudal society.

Second, after the Germans conquered Rome, they did not initially start to develop feudalism, but slavery which was already developed within Rome. This was because they were more familiar with the slavery system than with feudalism. As dictated by the development of Germanic society, the Germanic kings and nobles wanted to develop slavery in Rome after their conquest of Rome. In fact, in the various kingdoms established by Germans, relations of production of slavery were widespread. For example, poor freeholders often sold themselves and their children into slavery. The government of the Eastern Gothic Kingdom passed legislation to safeguard the exploitation and oppression of slaves by the Germanic and Roman nobles. It stipulated that slaves were completely owned by their masters. Fugitive slaves would be arrested and returned to the owner, and slaves were strictly forbidden from suing their masters. During the Merovingian Dynasty under the Frankish Kingdom, the number of slaves was for a time more than that before the fall of the Western Roman Empire. In addition to the slaves of the Roman era, a large number became slaves from being previous war prisoners or due to debts or crimes. The slave trade was quite prosperous. The status of slaves was very low. Salic law stipulated that, to kill a slave, you only need to compensate the master for the price of a horse. However, social forms do not shift according to anyone's subjective will. At that time, slavery was in decline and severely hindered the development of productive forces. It was impossible to revive a slavery society and a slavery state at the time. Thus, the Germans had to give up slavery. Instead, they established a feudal system based on existing feudal forces in Rome. This fully shows that the feudal system of the Middle Ages in Western Europe was established not only on the basis of Roman slavery, but also on slavery that had emerged and very much matured among the German conquerors. Slavery was the inevitable stage before the feudal system. In a letter to Marx on December 16, 1882, Engels referred to the feudal system of the ninth to 11th centuries A.D. in these words, "when the old Germanic slavery still continued."[47] This illustrates the change from a slave society to a feudal society.

Based on the productive forces developed under Roman slavery, Germans established feudalism after conquering the Roman Empire. Marxism believes that productive forces are the most active and revolutionary factor in production. A certain level of the productive forces always requires corresponding relations of production. This is the objective law independent of human will. After conquering the Roman Empire, Germans could not continue slavery, but had to establish feudalism, as ultimately determined not by political violence, nor by their wills, but by the prevailing level of productivity. Marx and Engels thus talked about the Germanic conquest of the Roman Empire in *The German Ideology*:

> It follows that the form of community adopted by the settling conquerors must correspond to the stage of development of the productive forces they find in existence; or, if this is not the case from the start, it must change according to the productive forces. By this, too, is explained the fact, which people profess to have noticed everywhere in the period following the migration of the peoples, namely, that the servant was master, and that the conquerors very soon took over language, culture and manners from the conquered.[48]

Marx and Engels summed up the historical process in which the Germanic people attempted to develop slavery after conquering Rome, but instead had to establish and develop feudalism because slavery would have violated the development requirements of the prevailing productive forces. Marx and Engels continue:

> The feudal system was by no means brought complete from Germany, but had its origin, as far as the conquerors were concerned, in the martial organisation of the army during the actual conquest, and this only evolved after the conquest into the feudal system proper through the action of the productive forces found in the conquered countries. To what an extent this form was determined by the productive forces is shown by the abortive attempts to realise other forms derived from reminiscences of ancient Rome (Charlemagne, etc.).[49]

In *Anti-Dühring*, Engels also said:

> Every conquest by a more barbarian people disturbs of course the economic development and destroys numerous productive forces. But in the immense majority of cases where the conquest is permanent, the more barbarian

> conqueror has to adapt himself to the higher 'economic situation' as it emerges from the conquest; he is assimilated by the vanquished and in most cases he has even to adopt their language.[50]

This shows that the establishment of feudalism must be based on the developed productive forces current within the slavery. In other words, due to the productive forces matured by slavery, only feudalism could be established. If other social systems were forced, they would have destroyed the prevailing productive forces and, at the end of the day, would have resulted in having to revert back to feudalism. This again illustrates the process of transformation from a slave society to a feudal society.

In *The German Ideology*, Marx and Engels criticized the fallacy that the conquest of one nation by another is the root cause of the change in social forms. They said:

> Nothing is more common than the notion that in history up till now it has only been a question of taking. The barbarians take the Roman Empire, and this fact of taking is made to explain the transition from the old world to the feudal system. In this taking by barbarians, however, the question is, whether the nation which is conquered has evolved industrial productive forces, as is the case with modern peoples, or whether their productive forces are based for the most part merely on their association and on the community. Taking is further determined by the object taken. A banker's fortune, consisting of paper, cannot be taken at all, without the taker's submitting to the conditions of production and intercourse of the country taken. Similarly, the total industrial capital of a modern industrial country. And finally, everywhere there is very soon an end to taking, and when there is nothing more to take, you have to set about producing.[51]

This shows that the root cause of social changes is neither political violence nor the conquest of one nation by another, but improvement of the productive forces.

Notes

1 Jiang Yihua & Wu Kequan (1991). *A Contending Series of Social Sciences – History Volume*. Shanghai, China: Shanghai People's Publishing House, 133–138.
2 Li Hongzhe (1957). Is "Slave Society" the Unavoidable Stage of Social Development. *Literature, History and Philosophy*, Vol. 10.
3 Wu Yuqin & Qi Shirong (Eds.) (1994). *World History—Ancient History Series*. Beijing, China: Higher Education Press, 176–177.
4 Wu Yuqin & Qi Shirong (Eds.) (1994). *World History—Ancient History Series*. Beijing, China: Higher Education Press, 144.
5 Wu Yuqin & Qi Shirong (Eds.) (1994). *World History—Ancient History Series*. Beijing, China: Higher Education Press, 178.
6 Wu Yuqin & Qi Shirong (Eds.) (1994). *World History—Ancient History Series*. Beijing, China: Higher Education Press, 187.

7 *An Anthology of Marx and Engels* (Vol. 7). (2009). Beijing, China: People's Publishing House, 894.
8 *An Anthology of Marx and Engels* (Vol. 7). (2009). Beijing, China: People's Publishing House, 894–895.
9 *An Anthology of Marx and Engels* (Vol. 7). (2009). Beijing, China: People's Publishing House, 893.
10 Wu Yuqin & Qi Shirong (Eds.) (1994). *World History—Ancient History Series*. Beijing, China: Higher Education Press, 263–264.
11 *An Anthology of Marx and Engels* (Vol. 4). (2009). Beijing, China: People's Publishing House, 136.
12 *An Anthology of Marx and Engels* (Vol. 4). (2009). Beijing, China: People's Publishing House, 136.
13 *Collected Works of Marx and Engels* (Vol. 4). (1995). Beijing, China: People's Publishing House, 33.
14 *Collected Works of Lenin* (Vol. 55). (1990). Beijing, China: People's Publishing House, 296.
15 *An Anthology of Marx and Engels* (Vol. 9). (2009). Beijing, China: People's Publishing House, 439.
16 *An Anthology of Marx and Engels* (Vol. 8). (2009). Beijing, China: People's Publishing House, 36.
17 *An Anthology of Marx and Engels* (Vol. 9). (2009). Beijing, China: People's Publishing House, 188.
18 Wu Yuqin & Qi Shirong (Eds.) (1994). *World History—Ancient History Series*. Beijing, China: Higher Education Press, 358–359.
19 Wu Yuqin & Qi Shirong (Eds.) (1994). *World History—Ancient History Series*. Beijing, China: Higher Education Press, 359.
20 Yuan Xingpei (2006). *History of Chinese Civilisation*. (Vol. 1). Beijing, China: Peking University Press, 229–230.
21 Du Shiran (1982). *A History of Science and Technology in China*. Beijing, China: Science Press, 314–315.
22 Yuan Xingpei (2006). *History of Chinese Civilisation*. (Vol.1). Beijing, China: Peking University Press, 234–236.
23 Du Shiran (1982). *A History of Science and Technology in China*. Beijing, China: Science Press, 314–315.
24 Needham, J. (2010). *Science and Civilization in China* (staff at Science History Department of Shanghai Jiaotong University Trans.). Shanghai, China: Shanghai People's Publishing House, 265–266.
25 *Selected Works of Mao Zedong* (Vol. 2). (1991). Beijing, China: People's Publishing House, 617.
26 *Collected Works of Marx and Engels* (Vol. 47). (1979). Beijing, China: People's Publishing House, 427.
27 *An Anthology of Marx and Engels* (Vol. 7). (2009). Beijing, China: People's Publishing House, 895.
28 *An Anthology of Marx and Engels* (Vol. 7). (2009). Beijing, China: People's Publishing House, 898.
29 *An Anthology of Marx and Engels* (Vol. 7). (2009). Beijing, China: People's Publishing House, 900–902.
30 Ma Keyao (Ed.) (2004). *History of the World Civilization*. (Vol. 1). Beijing, China: Peking University Press, 204.
31 *Selected Works of Mao Zedong* (Vol. 2). (1991). Beijing, China: People's Publishing House, 625.
32 Ma Keyao (Ed.) (2004). *History of the World Civilization*. (Vol. 1). Beijing, China: Peking University Press, 335.
33 Umberto Melotti (1981). *Marx and the Third World* (Gao Xian et al. Trans.). Beijing, China: The Commercial Press, 63.

34 Zhang Chuanxi (1961). The Formation and Establishment of Feudal Land Ownership in Pre-Han Period. *Peking University Journal*, Vol. 2. 23–31.
35 Zhu Huan (1996). *A Comparative Study on the Feudal Economic Forms of Asia and Europe*. Changchun, China: Northeast Normal University Press, 238–273.
36 *An Anthology of Marx and Engels* (Vol. 2). (2009). Beijing, China: People's Publishing House, 564, 566.
37 *An Anthology of Marx and Engels* (Vol. 3). (2009). Beijing, China: People's Publishing House, 151–152, 153, 154.
38 Ma Keyao (1982). Understanding the "Feudalization" in Europe. *Historical Research*, Vol.4: 37–43.
39 Liu Xiuming (1981). The Typicality of China's Feudal Society and Reasons for Its Longevity. *Historical Research*, Vol. 6: 59–68.
40 Wang Zhengping (1981). On Reasons and Common Features for Some Nations to Transit to the Feudal Society Directly. *Historical Research*, Vol. 2: 29–42.
41 Cheng Chun & Shen Minhua (1981). On Western Europe's Transition from Slave Society to Feudal Society. *Historical Research*, Vol.1: 21–29.
42 *An Anthology of Marx and Engels* (Vol. 4). (2009). Beijing, China: People's Publishing House, 168–169.
43 Cheng Chun & Shen Minhua (1981). A Study of Western Europe's Transition from Slavery to Feudalism. *Historical Research*, Vol.1: 21–29.
44 Chen Zhaozhang (1979). On Productive Forces and Relations of Production in Western Europe's Feudal Society. *Journal of Xiamen University*, Vol. 4: 102–115.
45 Chen Zhaozhang (1979). On Productive Forces and Relations of Production in Western Europe's Feudal Society. *Journal of Xiamen University*, Vol. 4: 102–115.
46 *An Anthology of Marx and Engels* (Vol. 1). (2009). Beijing, China: People's Publishing House, 522.
47 *Collected Works of Marx and Engels* (Vol. 35). (1971). Beijing, China: People's Publishing House, 125.
48 *An Anthology of Marx and Engels* (Vol. 9). (2009). Beijing, China: People's Publishing House, 191.
49 *An Anthology of Marx and Engels* (Vol. 1). (2009). Beijing, China: People's Publishing House, 578.
50 *An Anthology of Marx and Engels* (Vol. 9). (2009). Beijing, China: People's Publishing House, 191.
51 *An Anthology of Marx and Engels* (Vol. 1). (2009). Beijing, China: People's Publishing House, 578.

Bibliography

Classic works of Marxism

1. *An Anthology of Marx and Engels* (Vols. 1–10). (2009). Beijing, China: People's Publishing House.
2. *Collected Works of Marx and Engels* (Vol. 1). (1955). Beijing, China: People's Publishing House.
3. *Collected Works of Marx and Engels* (Vol. 3). (1960). Beijing, China: People's Publishing House.
4. *Collected Works of Marx and Engels* (Vol. 19). (1963). Beijing, China: People's Publishing House.
5. *Collected Works of Marx and Engels* (Vol. 20). (1971). Beijing, China: People's Publishing House.
6. *Collected Works of Marx and Engels* (Vol. 28). (1973). Beijing, China: People's Publishing House.
7. *Collected Works of Marx and Engels* (Vol. 32). (1974). Beijing, China: People's Publishing House.
8. *Collected Works of Marx and Engels* (Vol. 33). (1973). Beijing, China: People's Publishing House.
9. *Collected Works of Marx and Engels* (Vol. 35). (1971). Beijing, China: People's Publishing House.
10. *Collected Works of Marx and Engels* (Vol. 39). (1974). Beijing, China: People's Publishing House.
11. *Collected Works of Marx and Engels* (Vol. 1). (1995). Beijing, China: People's Publishing House.
12. *Collected Works of Marx and Engels* (Vol. 3). (2002). Beijing, China: People's Publishing House.
13. *Collected Works of Marx and Engels* (Vol. 21). (2003). Beijing, China: People's Publishing House.
14. *Collected Works of Marx and Engels* (Vol. 30). (1995). Beijing, China: People's Publishing House.
15. *Collected Works of Marx and Engels* (Vol. 31). (1998). Beijing, China: People's Publishing House.
16. *Collected Works of Marx and Engels* (Vol. 32). (1998). Beijing, China: People's Publishing House.

17. *Collected Works of Marx and Engels* (Vol. 33). (2004). Beijing, China: People's Publishing House.
18. *Collected Works of Marx and Engels* (Vol. 34). (2008). Beijing, China: People's Publishing House.
19. *Collected Works of Lenin* (Vol. 1). (1984). Beijing, China: People's Publishing House.
20. *Collected Works of Lenin* (Vol. 10). (1987). Beijing, China: People's Publishing House.
21. *Collected Works of Lenin* (Vol. 11). (1987). Beijing, China: People's Publishing House.
22. *Collected Works of Lenin* (Vol. 12). (1987). Beijing, China: People's Publishing House.
23. *Collected Works of Lenin* (Vol. 32). (1985). Beijing, China: People's Publishing House.
24. *Collected Works of Lenin* (Vol. 33). (1985). Beijing, China: People's Publishing House.
25. *Collected Works of Lenin* (Vol. 34). (1985). Beijing, China: People's Publishing House.
26. *Collected Works of Lenin* (Vol. 35). (1985). Beijing, China: People's Publishing House.
27. *Collected Works of Lenin* (Vol. 36). (1985). Beijing, China: People's Publishing House.
28. *Collected Works of Lenin* (Vol. 37). (1986). Beijing, China: People's Publishing House.
29. *Collected Works of Lenin* (Vol. 38). (1986). Beijing, China: People's Publishing House.
30. *Collected Works of Lenin* (Vol. 40). (1986). Beijing, China: People's Publishing House.
31. *Collected Works of Lenin* (Vol. 41). (1986). Beijing, China: People's Publishing House.
32. *Collected Works of Lenin* (Vol. 42). (1987). Beijing, China: People's Publishing House.
33. *Collected Works of Lenin* (Vol. 43). (1987). Beijing, China: People's Publishing House.
34. *Collected Works of Lenin* (Vol. 55). (1990). Beijing, China: People's Publishing House.
35. *Selected Works of Lenin* (Vols. 1–4). (1995). Beijing, China: People's Publishing House.
36. *Selected Works of Marx and Engels* (Vols. 1–4). (1995). Beijing, China: People's Publishing House.

Chinese literature

37. Ailin, Luo (2007). *Research on Rural Communities in the Late Feudal Society of Russia*. Guilin, China: Guangxi Normal University Press.
38. Central Compilation and Translation Bureau & International Communist Movement History Research Office (Eds.) (1983). *Russian Populist Anthology*. Beijing, China: People's Publishing House.

39. Central Compilation and Translation Bureau (Ed.) (1996). *Notes on Marx's Ancient Social History*. Beijing, China: People's Publishing House.
40. Editing Group of *Introduction to Scientific Socialism*. (2011). *Introduction to Scientific Socialism*. Beijing, China: People's Publishing House and Higher Education Press.
41. Falu, Yin, et al. (Eds.) (2008). *Ancient Chinese Cultural History* (Illustrated edition) (Vols. 1–2). Beijing, China: Peking University Press.
42. Gang, Feng (1992). *Non-Western Theory of Social Development and Marx*. Zhejiang, China: Zhejiang People's Publishing House.
43. Huan, Zhu (Ed.) (1996). *A Comparative Study on the Feudal Economic Forms of Asia and Europe*. Changchun, China: Northeast Normal University Press.
44. Jianjin, Zhu (1996). *Where Does the Eastern Society Go—Marx's Theory of the Eastern Society*. Shanghai, China: Shanghai Academy of Social Sciences Press.
45. Keyao, Ma (Ed.) (2004). *History of World Civilization* (Vols. 1–2). Beijing, China: Peking University Press.
46. Lei, Yuan, & Zhang, Yunfei (2013). *Marx and Engels on the "Oriental Village Community": A Research Reader*. Beijing, China: Central Compilation & Translation Press.
47. Liangzao, Yu (2011). *Marx's Orientalism*. Beijing, China: People's Publishing House.
48. Liangzao, Yu, & Xu, Qin (2015). *Classical Works and Fundamental Theories on Social Development in Eastern Backward Countries*. Beijing, China: People's Publishing House.
49. Lin, Xie (1992). *The Road to Oriental Society*. Beijing, China: China Social Sciences Press.
50. Longhua, Zhu (1991). *World History—Ancient Part*. Beijing, China: Peking University Press.
51. Qiliang, Liu (1994). *Marx's Theory of the Oriental Society*. Shanghai, China: Xuelin Press.
52. Shiran, Du et al. (1984). *A History of Science and Technology in China* (Vols. 1–2). Beijing, China: Science Press.
53. Wailu, Hou (1979). *On the History of Chinese Feudal Society*. Beijing, China: People's Publishing House.
54. Wailu, Hou (2003). *On the History of Ancient Chinese Society*. Shijiazhuang, China: Hebei Education Press.
55. Weian, Cao (2002). *New theory of Russian History—Basic Issues Affecting the Development of Russian History*. Beijing, China: China Social Sciences Press.
56. Xianda, Chen (1987). *To the Depths of History—A Study of Marx's View of History*. Shanghai, China: Shanghai People's Publishing House.
57. Xingpei, Yuan, et al. (Eds.) (2006). *History of Chinese Civilization* (Vols. 1–4). Beijing, China: Peking University Press.
58. Yan, Jin, & Qin, Hui (2013). *Rural Commune, Reform and Revolution—Village Community Tradition and the Road to Russian Modernization*. Beijing, China: The Eastern Publishing Co., Ltd.
59. Yue, Lu, et al. (1992). *The Creative Exploration of Marx in His Later Years—On "Anthropological Notes"*. Zhengzhou, China: Henan People's Publishing House.
60. Yuqin, Wu, & Qi, Shirong (Eds.) (1994). *World History—Ancient History Series*. Beijing, China: Higher Education Press.
61. Zhenhua, Hao (Ed.) (1981). *Foreign Scholars on the Asiatic Mode of Production* (Vols. 1–2). Beijing, China: China Social Sciences Press.

Other literature: translations

62. Appianus, A. (1976). *Roman History* (Vols. 1–2) (Xie Defeng Trans.). Beijing, China: The Commercial Press.
63. Bentley, J., & Ziegler, H. (2007). *Traditions & Encounters* (Vols. 1–2) (3rd ed.) (Wei Fenglian et al. Trans.). Beijing, China: Peking University Press.
64. Hegel, G. W. F. (1956). *Historical Philosophy* (Wang Zaoshi Trans.). Shanghai, China: SDX Joint Publishing Company.
65. Hegel, G. W. F. (1980). *The Shorter Logic* (He Lin Trans.). Beijing, China: The Commercial Press.
66. Marx, K. H., & Engels, F. (1987). *Marx and Engels' Correspondence with Russian Political Activists* (Ma Yiruo et al. Trans.). Beijing, China: People's Publishing Press.
67. Melotti, U. (1981). *Marx and the Third World* (Gao Xian et al. Trans.). Beijing, China: The Commercial Press.
68. Montesquieu, C. (1961). *The Spirit of the Laws* (Vols. 1–2) (Zhang Yanshen Trans.). Beijing, China: The Commercial Press.
69. Morgan, L. H. (1977). *Ancient Society* (Vols. 1–2) (Yang Dongchun Trans.). Beijing, China: The Commercial Press.
70. Needham, J. (2010). *Science and Civilization in China* (staff at Science History Department of Shanghai Jiaotong University Trans.). Shanghai, China: Shanghai People's Publishing House.
71. Rousseau, J. J. (2009). *On the Origin of Human Inequality* (Lü Zhuo Trans.). Beijing, China: China Social Sciences Press.
72. Rousseau, J. J. (2009). *The Social Contract* (Xu Qiang Trans.). Beijing, China: China Social Sciences Press.
73. Smith, A. (1997). *The Theory of Moral Sentiments* (Jiang Ziqiang et al. Trans.). Beijing, China: The Commercial Press.
74. Smith, A. (2001). *An Inquiry into the Nature and Causes of the Wealth of Nations* (Yang Jingnian Trans.). Xi'an, China: Shaanxi People's Publishing House.
75. Spengler, O. (1963). *The Decline of the West* (Vols. 1–2) (Qi Shirong et al. Trans.). Beijing, China: The Commercial Press.
76. Stavrianos, L. S. (2005). *A Global History–From Prehistory to the 21st Century* (7th ed.) (Vols. 1–2) (Dong Shuhui et al. Trans.). Beijing, China: Peking University Press.
77. Thucydides, A. (1960). *History of the Peloponnesian War* (Vols. 1–2) (Xie Defeng Trans.). Beijing, China: The Commercial Press.
78. Toynbee, A. (1964). *A Study of History* (Vols. 1–3) (Cao Mofeng et al. Trans.). Shanghai, China: Shanghai People's Publishing House.
79. Vico, G. (1989). *New Science* (Zhu Guangqian Trans.). Beijing, China: The Commercial Press.

Foreign literature

80. Bernier, F. (1916). *Travels in the Mogul Empire* (English version). Oxford, England: Oxford University Press.

Index

Taylor & Francis Group
an informa business

Taylor & Francis eBooks

www.taylorfrancis.com

A single destination for eBooks from Taylor & Francis with increased functionality and an improved user experience to meet the needs of our customers.

90,000+ eBooks of award-winning academic content in Humanities, Social Science, Science, Technology, Engineering, and Medical written by a global network of editors and authors.

TAYLOR & FRANCIS EBOOKS OFFERS:

A streamlined experience for our library customers

A single point of discovery for all of our eBook content

Improved search and discovery of content at both book and chapter level

REQUEST A FREE TRIAL

support@taylorfrancis.com

Routledge
Taylor & Francis Group

CRC Press
Taylor & Francis Group

For Product Safety Concerns and Information please contact our EU representative GPSR@taylorandfrancis.com
Taylor & Francis Verlag GmbH, Kaufingerstraße 24, 80331 München, Germany

www.ingramcontent.com/pod-product-compliance
Lightning Source LLC
LaVergne TN
LVHW021113300926
849160LV00009B/722
* 9 7 8 1 0 3 2 3 3 6 0 5 3 *